Dream

Also by Stephen Duncombe

The Bobbed Haired Bandit:
A True Story of Crime and Celebrity in 1920s New York
(co-authored with Andrew Mattson)

The Cultural Resistance Reader *(editor)*

Notes from Underground:
Zines and the Politics of Alternative Culture

Dream

Re-imagining Progressive Politics
in an Age of Fantasy

Stephen Duncombe

THE NEW PRESS

NEW YORK
LONDON

Published in the United States by The New Press, New York, 2007
Distributed by W. W. Norton & Company, Inc., New York

LIBRARY OF CONGRESS CATALOGING-IN-PUBLICATION DATA

Duncombe, Stephen.
    Dream: re-imagining progressive politics in an age of fantasy / Stephen Duncombe.
    p. cm.
    Includes bibliographical references and index.
    ISBN-13: 978-1-59558-049-8 (hc.)
    ISBN-10: 1-59558-049-2 (hc.)
    1. Political participation—United States. 2. Progressivism (United States politics)
    3. United States—Politics and government—2001– I. Title.
    JK1764.D863 2007
    320.51'30973—dc22
    2006012056

The New Press was established in 1990 as a not-for-profit alternative to the large, commercial publishing houses currently dominating the book publishing industry. The New Press operates in the public interest rather than for private gain, and is committed to publishing, in innovative ways, works of educational, cultural, and community value that are often deemed insufficiently profitable.

www.thenewpress.com

Book design by Rob Carmichael, SEEN
This book was set in Caecilia and Goudy Sans

Printed in the United States of America

10 9 8 7 6 5 4 3 2 1

For it must be noted that men must either be caressed or else annihilated.   —Niccolò Machiavelli, 1532

So long as you rely on the efficacy of "scientific" demonstrations and logical proof you can hold your [political] convention in anybody's back parlor and have room to spare.   —Walter Lippmann, 1913

All power to the imagination!   —Graffiti in Paris, May 1968

In our dreams we have seen another world. . . . And this new, true world was not a dream from the past; it was not something that came from our ancestors. It came to us from the future; it was the next step that we had to take.   —Subcomandante Marcos, 1994

Contents

Acknowledgments

This book arose out of many discussions and demonstrations. To begin, I'd like to thank everyone in the *Fantasy Reäl* cabal for their wisdom, criticism, and good company, and to single out two members in particular: Jeremy Varon, for his insightful and encouraging correspondence over the course of this book, and Andrew Boyd, for the brainstorming sessions that got it going in the first place. In addition, Andrew generously allowed me to cannibalize and reprint fragments of an earlier essay we co-wrote.

I want to thank my political comrades in the Lower East Side Collective, Reclaim the Streets, Absurd Response, the Clandestine Insurgent Rebel Clown Army, and so many other groups, who have taught me so much over the years. In addition, Larry Bogad, Jane Duncombe, Jason Grote, Ron Hayduk, Leslie Kauffman, Andrew Mattson, Kelley Moore, Mark Read, Chuck "Yeo" Reinhardt, Ben Shepard, Astra Taylor, and Alice Meaker Varon have influenced my thinking on this project. I'd like to thank all my colleagues at the Gallatin School of New York University, particularly Ali Mirsepassi for his support, Mary Witty for making the chair's work manage-able, Nina Cornyetz for her knowledge of all things Fascist, George Shulman for sharpening my thinking about dreaming, Lisa Goldfarb for raising the politics of poetry, and Michael Dinwiddie for keeping me sane on Saturday mornings. I want to thank my students, specifically Stacy Han, Kavita Kulkarni, Kavita Rajanna, and Geoffrey Winder for keeping my thinking fresh; my "game boys" Robert Jones, Oren Ross, and especially Haim Schoppik and Ivan Askwith for their help in understanding—and playing—*Grand Theft Auto*; Maryellen Strautmanis and Sofia Contreras for taking such good care of my own boys; Eyal Rozmarin for sharing his passion for theory and his understanding of the intersection of politics and psychology (including mine); and the staff of Café Esperanto on MacDougal Street, my office away from my office, for putting up with my long lingerings over a single cup of coffee.

I will always be indebted to my mentor Stuart Ewen for intro-ducing me to the works of Walter Lippmann and teaching me about the importance of spectacle—though I'm not quite certain I learned the lessons he intended. I am also much obliged to *The Baffler*, the *Journal of Aesthetics and Protest*, the *Brooklyn Rail*, and *Radical Society* for letting me try out some of these ideas in print and then allowing me to borrow them back. Thanks go to Colin Robinson for his instinct for the audacious and for his generous embrace of my ideas, first at Verso and then at The New Press; Andy Hsiao for his encouragement; Stewart Cauley for his graphic sense; Maury Botton for putting this all together; Ina Howard for spreading the word; and my editor, Sarah Fan, who got this book from the beginning and then worked hard to get it where it needed to go. Also, a very special thanks go out to my father, the Reverend David C. Duncombe, who has shown me throughout his life that politics must speak to more than just the mind. And finally, none of this would have been possible without the love and advice of my wife and unofficial editor, Jean Railla. This book is dedicated to our two sons, Sydney and Sebastien, who, more than anyone else, have taught me the power of imagination.

1. Politics in an Age of Fantasy

In the autumn of 2004, shortly before the U.S. presidential election and in the middle of a typically bloody month in Iraq, the *New York Times Magazine* ran a feature article on the casualty of truth in the Bush administration. Like most *Times* articles, it was well written, well researched, and thoroughly predictable. That George W. Bush is ill informed, doesn't listen to dissenting opinion, and acts upon whatever nonsense he happens to believe is hardly news. (Even the fact that he once insisted that Sweden did not have an army and none of his cabinet dared contradict him was not all that surprising.) There was, however, one valuable insight. In a soon-to-be-infamous passage, the writer, Ron Suskind, recounted a conversation between himself and an unnamed senior adviser to the president:

> The aide said that guys like me were "in what we call the reality-based community," which he defined as people who "believe that solutions emerge from your judicious study of discernable reality." I nodded and murmured something about Enlightenment principles

and empiricism. He cut me off. "That's not the way the world really works anymore," he continued. "We're an empire now, and when we act, we create reality. And while you are studying that reality— judiciously, as you will—we'll act again creating other new realities, which you can study too, and that's how things will sort out. We're history's actors . . . and you, all of you, will be left to just study what we do.[1]

It was clear how the *Times* felt about this peek into the political mind of the presidency. The editors of the Gray Lady pulled out the passage and floated it over the article in oversized, multi-colored type. This was ideological gold: the Bush administration openly and arrogantly admitting that they didn't care about reality. One could almost feel the palpable excitement generated among the *Times* liberal readership, an enthusiasm mirrored and amplified all down the left side of the political spectrum on computer listservs, call-in radio shows, and print editorials over the next few weeks.[2] This proud assertion of naked disregard for reality and unbounded faith in fantasy was the most damning evidence of Bush insanity yet. He must surely lose the election now.

What worried me then, and still worries me today, is that my reaction was radically different. My politics have long been diametrically opposed to those of the Bush administration, and I've had a long career as a left-leaning academic and a progressive political activist. Yet I read the same words that generated so much animosity among liberals and the left and felt something else: excited, inspired . . . and jealous. Whereas the commonsense view held that Bush's candid disregard for reality was evidence of the madness of his administration, I perceived it as a much more disturbing sign of its brilliance. I knew then that Bush, in spite of making a mess of nearly everything he had undertaken in his first presidential term, would be reelected.

How could my reaction be so different from that of so many of my colleagues and comrades? Maybe I was becoming a neocon, another addition to the long list of defectors whose progressive God had failed. Would I follow the path of Christopher Hitchens? A truly depressing thought. But what if, just maybe, the problem was not with me but with the main currents of progressive thinking in this country? More precisely, maybe there was something about progressive politics that had become increasingly problematic.

The problem, as I see it, comes down to reality. Progressives believe in it, Bush's people believe in creating it. The left and right have switched roles—the right taking on the mantle of radicalism and progressives waving the flag of conservatism. The political progeny of the protestors who proclaimed, "Take your desires for reality" in May of 1968, were now counseling the reversal: take reality for your desires.[3] Republicans were the ones proclaiming, "I have a dream."

Dreams often make those who are left-of-center nervous. Fantasy and spectacle have been the property of Fascism, totalitarian Communism, and, more recently, the unspeakable horror known as *Entertainment Tonight*. Traditionally we are more comfortable with those things mumbled by the *Times* reporter underneath his breath: "Enlightenment principles and empiricism." But what are these things in which liberals put so much faith? Empiricism, put simply, is the theory that things exist and can be measured independently of those doing the measuring. There are facts to be discovered and truth to be discerned, if only we can separate out the desires of people. In the early 1600s the pioneering scientist Galileo Galilei wrote of the necessity of distinguishing qualities that "exist in external bodies" and can be measured—size, shape, quantity, and motion—from qualities like color, smell, and taste, which are subjective judgments. The former have an autonomous and verifiable reality, while the latter "exist only in the sensitive body, for when the living creature is removed all these qualities are carried off and annihilated." These latter, all-too-human impressions are, in Galileo's wonderful phrase, "nothing more than mere names."[4] The job of science, then, is to hold human subjectivity in check in order to reveal the objective reality that precedes it. Reality, once freed from tradition and superstition and no longer clouded by imagination and emotion, is self-evident.

Self-evident reality was critical to the Enlightenment as well. Philosophers of the Enlightenment—the name bestowed upon a loose school of thought centered in Europe around the 1700s—believed that politics should strive to model itself upon the "real" of the world, including the real nature of man. For Thomas Hobbes, man was brutish and cruel; for Jean-Jacques Rousseau, he was noble and good; yet both held that any system of just and lasting governance must base itself upon this revealed "real." That is, politics must be based in fact, not mere tradition or superstition. Another key tenet of Enlightenment thought followed from this. Man, in order to reveal this "real" and act upon it accordingly, must be able to reason and act rationally. Just as an empiricist astronomer could examine the trajectory of a planet without reference to heavenly bodies, the citizen imagined by the Enlightenment had the ability to discern the forces governing his or her life and make thoughtful decisions based upon the (judicious) study of such observations. Through reason a citizenry could intelligently choose one leader, policy, or system of government over the other. As a rational actor, *homo economicus* guided the invisible hand of the market. Reason and rationality, so the theory goes, were and are the cornerstones of democracy and capitalism.

It is not surprising that progressives feel an affinity for the Enlightenment and empiricism. It was empiricism that broke the Church's grip on the interpretation of the world. By challenging the Church on its explanations of the physical world, the empiricists opened up an assault on its political and spiritual power as well. Likewise, the Enlightenment ideal of man as a rational, reasoning creature undermined the hierarchies of feudalism and the foundations of divine right. Traditional "common sense" held that common people could not govern themselves nor act orderly in the marketplace. Contesting these assumptions cleared the way for new forms of politics and economics.[5] The religious festivals and entertaining spectacles mobilized by Church and crown to excite or divert the masses and cement religious or royal power could now be replaced by town meetings and coffeehouses where enlightened citizens debated the issues of the day. These reasonable citizens, understanding reality as it is and not as it is imagined, would guide democracy and rationalize the market, breaking forever with a reactionary past cloaked in magic, mystery, and manipulation. In other words, and more to the point, progressives throughout history embraced the Enlightenment and empiricism because historically these ideas were progressive.[6]

But all this is history. Appeals to truth and reality, and faith in rational thought and action, are based in a fantasy of the past, or rather, past fantasy.[7] Today's world is linked by media systems and awash in advertising images; political policies are packaged by public relations experts and celebrity gossip is considered news. More and more of the economy is devoted to marketing and entertainment or the performance of scripted roles in the service sector.[8] We live in a "society of the spectacle," as the French theorist-provocateur Guy Debord declared back in 1967. Yet, faced with this new world, progressives are still acting out a script inherited from the past. This is a mistake, for those who put their trust in Enlightenment principles and empiricism today are doomed to political insignificance.[9]

This is largely where liberals and the left reside now. Consider the recent ghoulish spectacle of Terri Schiavo, the brain-dead woman kept alive by forced medical feeding against the wishes of her husband and the decisions of a court. In a roundabout effort to inch toward outlawing abortion, conservative politicians dramatized the tragedy as an epic struggle of the right to life, of the lofty primacy of the spirit over the body. Politician stood shoulder to shoulder with priest in an appeal for state intervention to prevent a helpless innocent from court-mandated death. It was grand theater, played to the hilt—despite opinion polls recording anywhere from 60 to 70 percent of Americans believing that government has no place in end-of-life decisions.[10] How did the Democrats capitalize on their opponents' popular weakness? With meek statements about proper judicial process and respect for expert medical opinion—all the inspiration of a Sergeant Friday: "Just the facts, ma'am. No need to get excited." This was not merely a case of political ineptitude; it was the manifestation of an Enlightenment-era faith that facts are more powerful than fantasies.

To be fair, there are some things that progressives do reasonably well. We reveal the lies of institutionalized power through investigative reporting and media exposure (Watergate, torture at Abu Ghraib prison). We demonstrate to those in power that "the whole world is watching" by marshalling hundreds of thousands of people for mass protests (the ritual "March on Washington"). And we influence privileged youth through our relative dominance in the universities (even though this victory is never acknowledged since doing so would mean admitting that what we teach is not simply the Truth). But these strengths are based upon a fundamental weakness: an Enlightenment faith that somehow, if reasoning people have access to the Truth, the scales will fall from their eyes and they will see reality as it truly is and, of course, agree with us.

To retain this faith, progressives have, ironically, closed their eyes to the reality of today's politico-cultural landscape. Despite repeated assertions that Saddam Hussein had nothing to do with al-Qaeda's terrorist attacks on 9/11 by nearly every respected news outlet in the United States (and even the not-so-respected governmental intelligence services), a majority of Americans believe there was a link. This is not some mass of illiterates living in a world where information is controlled by priests intoning in Latin. These are citizens of a highly literate nation awash in 24/7 information. Is there any better evidence that the problem is not one of access to the truth? The archaic concern with formal censorship has little validity in our age of informational overload.

Certainly U.S. propaganda gave the public's flight from facts a helping hand, but it was effective because the Pentagon understood that people often prefer a simple, dramatic story to the complicated truth. Weaned on endless advertisements, sitcoms, and Hollywood movies, we've learned to find comfort in compelling narratives and change the channel when confronted with messy facts. If Osama bin Laden is elusive and al-Qaeda ephemeral, Saddam Hussein and the easily recognized nation of Iraq seemed made for prime-time trouncing. When the Iraqis didn't welcome us as liberators, and catching Saddam proved anticlimactic, no matter: there was always *Saving Private Lynch*.

A climate of fear can fuel fantasy, as the Bush administration so effectively demonstrated in the days after the terrorist attacks on 9/11. When threatened and insecure, people will find a way to go with the story—no matter how irrational—that makes them feel safer. And it may be that the pull toward the dramatic is basic human modus operandi. Jesus, after all, used parables instead of rational arguments to get his points across in the Gospels. But today spectacle is center stage, driven by a mass media and a consumer economy that panders to and profits off of emotional narrative and the overhyped story. Once there were a few hold-outs: news, education, and so on. Now "fair and balanced" Fox is in the living room and commercially sponsored Channel One in the classroom. Spectacle is our way of making sense of the world. Truth and power belong to those who tell the better story.

Walter Lippmann, the influential writer, popular newspaper editor, and informal political adviser to nearly every president from Teddy Roosevelt to Lyndon Johnson, argued that democratic theory has little to do with democratic practice. Democratic theory resides in the coffeehouses and government buildings where enlightened men examine evidence, hold reasoned conversations, and arrive at rational decisions. Theoretical democracy is a heady process. Its practice aims a bit lower. To win elections among a large and diverse population and get the majority to agree upon policy or go along with decisions, politicians, like their commercial counterparts in Hollywood and on Madison Avenue, speak to people's fantasies and desires through a language of images and associations. By manipulating symbols, exploiting memories, and spinning stories, the political elite are able to guide the direction of public opinion. "The practice of democracy has turned a corner," Lippmann argued in his 1922 book *Public Opinion*, "A revolution is taking place, infinitely more significant than any shifting of economic power." He called this revolution the Manufacture of Consent.[11]

Those of us opposed to rule by a political elite learned an important lesson from Lippmann. If democracy is to be sustained, and citizens are to truly govern their lives, then the manufacture of consent must be continuously revealed and deconstructed. Political stagecraft must be relentlessly attacked with our arsenal of facts and reason.

We learned the wrong lesson.

Progressives should have learned to build a politics that embraces the dreams of people and fashions spectacles which give these fantasies form—a politics that understands desire and speaks to the irrational; a politics that employs symbols and associations; a politics that tells good stories. In brief, we should have learned to manufacture *dissent*.

We need to do this for strategic reasons. Whether one approves of it or not, fantasy and spectacle have become the lingua franca of our time. Progressives can talk all they want about the Bush administration's disregard for the truth and its dangerous flights of fancy, but no one other than the converted is listening. And when no one listens in a democracy, the alignment of power stays the same. If we want our ideas to lead and not trail the politics of this country, then we need to learn how to think and communicate in today's spectacular vernacular.

Recently, progressive political writers such as Thomas Frank have argued that if the Democratic Party is to have a political future, it needs to adopt platforms and embrace policies that materially benefit the majority of Americans. Frank is absolutely correct.[12] But unless the Democrats develop programs to sell these real material gains and employ strategies that acknowledge the more immaterial nature of citizens' hopes and dreams, they will continue to fail. With apologies to Galileo (who merely makes the mistake common to many modern Western thinkers), reality and fantasy don't inhabit separate spheres, they coexist and intermingle. Reality needs fantasy to render it desirable, just as fantasy needs reality to make it believable.

Progressive writers have pointed this out before, and a few are now being recognized. The cognitive linguist George Lakoff writes about how people use "conceptual categories and metaphors" to make sense of their world. These categories and metaphors allow us to translate hard information and direct experience into a conceptual form familiar and comfortable to us. As such, he argues, progressives need to think less about presenting facts and more about how to frame these facts in such a way that they make sense and hold meaning for everyday people.[13] Jim Wallis, a left-leaning evangelical Christian, argues for a "prophetic politics," a spiritually based politics which transcends pragmatic policy and moves beyond reasoned critique. Building upon the prophetic tradition of religion, Wallis believes that progressives must articulate an alternative vision of the world—that is, a dream of the future.[14]

These are excellent paths to take, but the journey needs to go much further. Framing issues is important, but expanding the definition of what a progressive frame might constitute is essential. Politically minded prophets have long employed divinely inspired dreams, but we need a secular alternative, dreams recognizable for what they are—human constructs of our hopes and desires— but no less powerful for their transparency.

Progressives, secular as well as religious, need to make peace with the less-than-rational nature of politics. This will take some effort, for it means rethinking an entire tradition of political thought. Aristotle, the uncontested philosophical father of our political tradition, barely mentions the irrational in the eight books of his seminal work *The Politics*. From his infamous arguments justifying slavery to the quirky sections on the influence of climate on the state, reason takes center stage. It is reason, after all, that distinguishes us as human. "Other creatures live by nature only; some live by habit to some extent. Man, however, lives by reason as well: he alone has reason."[15] In his writings on theater and rhetoric, the great philosopher recognizes the importance of the irrational, but in politics the topic is taboo.

Eventually, in an incomplete fragment on musical education in the conclusion of the final book of The Politics, Aristotle touches upon the irrational but does so only in the form of a warning: music can be dangerous to the state. Why? Because music (particularly the use of wind instruments and the "orgiastic and emotional" Phrygian music, which were the electric guitars and rock'n'roll of the classical period) spoke to the heart and body instead of the discerning mind.[16] Furthermore, such transcendent pleasure was the "feature common to all music, which appeals even to some animals and also to a great many slaves and children"—that is, music made disturbing alliances between citizens and noncitizens (and animals, so it seems) and threatened to undermine hierarchy and order.[17] It seems odd to end a treatise on politics with a warning about losing oneself in music—but also fitting, for Aristotle was giving voice to what has become a common political dream: the ideal state will have no place for dreaming.[18]

Later political theorists rejected Aristotle's lengthy defense of slavery and his slavish insistence on the "golden mean" in all things, but his deep suspicion of popular emotionality and the pleasures that can come from both producing and losing oneself in fantastical constructs, be they musical compositions or political demands, remains.[19] Liberal political theorists of the Enlightenment, such as Hobbes, Rousseau, and John Locke, the economist Adam Smith, and the statesman Thomas Jefferson, assumed the existence of a rational, reasoning being with the ability to enter into social contracts, political debates, and democratic self-governance. Their conservative opponents, such as French Revolution critic Edmund Burke and the reluctant American revolutionary Alexander Hamilton, argued that it was exactly because the people were not capable of reason that politics should be kept out of their hands. (Burke was particularly haunted by the specter of the French hairdresser making political decisions.)[20] Radicals in the Marxist tradition ingeniously incorporated both sides of the argument. They acknowledged the seemingly irrational behaviors of the majority of people who act against their own political interests by supporting the ruling class, but held out the promise of the masses' eventual awakening to "class consciousness" when, in the words of the *Communist Manifesto*, "man is at last compelled to face with sober senses, his real conditions of life, and his relations with his kind."[21] For all their ideological differences, these thinkers agreed on one thing: reason should rule.

Outside of politics, other realms of human life acknowledge and exalt the fantastic. Consider the texts of the great world religions: the Red Sea parting for Moses as the Jews flee to the promised land; the terrible beauty of Krishna as he advises Arjuna to kill his friends and kinsman in battle; the dissonant symbol of Jesus, the son of God, crucified on a cross like a common criminal; the lyrical cadences of the words of the Prophet Muhammad. The Hebrew Bible, the Bhagavad Gita, the New Testament, and the Koran are all quasipolitical models for right behavior and community relations, yet stripped of their narratives and symbols they would have no power to move their audience, and thus no power at all. How many stirring sermons use the endless genealogies, the begets and begottens, of the book of Numbers as source material?

Fantasy inspires the bulk of our entertainment as well: movies, television, popular music, video games, theme parks, casinos, strip clubs, and so on. No matter what their differences, each form of entertainment constitutes a sort of spectacle that promises to transport the spectator outside their present reality. Complaints about the unreal fantasies of Hollywood and the "lack of representation" in television sitcoms miss the function of entertainment: to escape the here and now, to imagine something different, something better.

While there are fundamentalists who insist on the literal truth of religious stories, and media activists who would like to make entertainment into a bleak mirror of our everyday lives, most of us are drawn toward religion and entertainment for very different reasons: because both address our desires and articulate our dreams. So why is politics exempt? One might think that particularly in politics, whose purpose is the organization and arrangement of people's lives, one might find the irrational front and center. But looking out over the wide expanse of Western political theory, the irrational is hard to spot. When it is noticed, it is treated as a contagion to quarantine or a disruption to manage, a stain on the otherwise clean landscape of reason.

But again, this is theory, and practice is something else entirely. Take national political conventions in the United States. In theory these conventions are meetings held "to discuss and decide important matters," according to the *Dictionary of Government and Politics*.[22] More specifically, the *American Political Dictionary* tells us a convention is "a meeting of party delegates . . . to decide on party policy and strategy and nominate candidates for elective office."[23] It is a reasoned process of discussion and decision and, finally, democratic action. But this, of course, is hooey. In conventions past, backroom deals were cut by political bosses in private smoke-filled suites and physical fights broke out among inebriated delegates on the convention floor.[24] This was bare-knuckles democracy. Today even that semblance of debate and discussion is gone. All decisions have already been made by the time the campaign button–bejeweled conventioneers invade their host cities. Illuminated by the bright lights of television, political conventions are floodlit stages on which to play out competing fantasies of the future of the country and its leader. The Republican candidate is presented as firm, resolute, and patriotic, awash in flags and martial symbols. The Democratic challenger conjures up the ideals of inclusion and opportunity, surrounded by faces of many races and stations. Or, as with the 2004 conventions, the parties swap fantasies; John Kerry played the war hero flanked by his Vietnam War Swift Boat comrades, a soldier-statesman leading a "Stronger America," while George W. Bush acted the down-home everyman surrounded by the Republican rainbow. The candidate's biopic, with its soft-focus images of candidate and country, packaged and produced months in advance, is the real star of the convention. The time when political parties decide instead to save money by staying at home and buying an hour's worth of prime-time TV space may not be too far off. It would be a much more efficient means to fulfill the real function of the modern political convention: a spectacle.

If progressives are to engage, rather than ignore, the phantas-magoric terrain of politics, we need to learn from those who do spectacle best: the architects of Las Vegas, video game designers, advertising's creative directors, and the producers and editors of celebrity media. This does not mean adopting flashy techniques to help us make sexier advertisements for progressive causes (though this wouldn't hurt). It means looking deep into the core of these and other examples of popular spectacle to divine exactly what makes them so popular.

The immense popularity of commercial culture needs to be acknowledged and respected. To get us to open our wallets, legions of very smart and very creative people make sure that what they produce resonates with our most powerful and intimate desires. There is a lot to learn here. Too often these sources of potential knowledge and inspiration are, at best, criticized and, at worst, ignored by progressives. This makes us feel better about our cultural sophistication, our "specialness," but it also keeps us powerless. The entertainment state should be ruthlessly criticized, but the techniques used to create and maintain it need to be enthusiastically explored and exploited for their progressive potential.

This entails looking deeper than the current vogue of celebrating commercial culture as a "site of resistance." Sure, people enjoy culture in unpredictable ways: some of us may read romance novels as feminist texts, others modify video games to create unauthorized versions or customize imported autos into street racers. In resisting the sanctioned rules for "right" consumption we experience the thrill of making mass culture our own. But the political efficacy of a resistance tied to the everyday use (or abuse) of a commercial product is debatable. There is a big difference between rereading reality and acting to make it anew. To not recognize this distinction is to confuse the everyday action of making meaning with the much rarer tasks of creation and transformation.[25] Furthermore, this sort of "resistance" is often cultivated by marketers who understand it—correctly—as another way to get consumers engaged with their product. Toyota's new Scion division, for example, makes consumer customization of their cars—or the "remix," as they call it—part of their marketing strategy, promoting this practice with the slogan "We relinquish all power to you."[26] Consumer culture always serves the needs of consumer capitalism, including making space for resistance when expedient or profitable.

Between arrogant rejection and populist acceptance of commercial culture lies a third approach: appropriating, co-opting, and, most important, *transforming* the techniques of spectacular capitalism into tools for social change. This is the fine art of transmutation, once practiced with great effect by the Church, which cleverly adopted components of pagan religions and forms of pagan ritual (the Christmas tree, for example) to do the work of Christianity.

To do this means recognizing that consumer culture—its crafted fantasies and stimulated desires—speaks to something deep and real within us. The American psychologist and pragmatist philosopher William James articulated this political strategy back in 1906 in a speech he gave to students at Stanford University on "The Moral Equivalent of War." The problem with pacifism, the pacifist James argued, was that it was presented in such a way as to seem weak and boring, a safe utopia where the lion lay down with the lamb. At their peril, pacifists ignored all the legitimate emotional needs that war fulfills: romance, valor, honor, and sacrifice. By not speaking to "the higher aspects of militaristic sentiment" in their appeals for peace, pacifists ignored the real passions that motivate people. The result was a contest between the vigor of Teddy Roosevelt and the pieties of a Sunday school teacher. The wars of the twentieth century loudly declared the winner. "Pacifists ought to enter more deeply into the aesthetical and ethical point of view of their opponents," James counseled, "*then move the point*, and your opponent will follow."[27] Progressives, long comfortable with disdaining and distancing themselves from impure desire, need to learn to speak to it, through it, with it . . . and then move the point.

This won't be easy. Spectacular culture is most often designed to manipulate people and take their money, not set the stage for liberty, equality, and fraternity. It often appeals to our worst traits, while reaching progressive goals depends upon our more generous instincts. It is understandable to worry that by recasting progressive politics within the terms of spectacle we will sacrifice our ethical strength. But the point is not to denude the progressive movement of its essential characteristics but to expand its possibilities, addressing a larger sector of the public by acknowledging, and working with, all the desires we possess. The challenge for progressives is to create ethical spectacles.

Progressive dreams, and the spectacles that give them tangible form, will look different than those conjured up by the Bush administration or the commercial directors of what critic Neil Gabler calls *Life, the Movie*.[28] Different not only in content—this should be obvious—but in form. Given the progressive ideals of egalitarianism and a politics that values the input of everyone, our dreamscapes will not be created by media-savvy experts of the left and then handed down to the rest of us to watch, consume, and believe. Instead, our spectacles will be participatory: dreams the public can mold and shape themselves. They will be active: spectacles that work only if people help create them. They will be open-ended: setting stages to ask questions and leaving silences to formulate answers. And they will be transparent: dreams that one knows are dreams but which still have power to attract and inspire. And, finally, the spectacles we create will not cover over or replace reality and truth but perform and amplify it.

Illusion may be a necessary part of political life, but delusion need not be. Progressives cannot sell the dream of a world with

no medical bills without backing it up with promises and policies that guarantee universal health care for every American. We
should not conjure up a utopia of pure skies and clean water unless we are serious about massive investment in alternative energy sources. To be certain, other sides don't have these qualms.
Bush gutted the Clean Air Act with his "Clear Skies Initiative," and
the oil companies fall over one another to tell us how green they
are, but such hypocrisy is unethical. It is also not effective. Sooner
or later myth and reality meet; witness the collapse of President
Bush's triumphal declaration of "Mission Accomplished" in the
face of daily casualties in Iraq.

I hope it is clear by now that my argument here is not some
postmodern provocation that the real does not exist.[29] Semantics
aside, there is an all-too-real "real" at hand: war in Iraq, growing national and world inequality, global warming and species
extinction—the list goes on. Make no mistake, there is an empirical real. But no matter how real this reality may be, it only means
something when we give it meaning.[30] As such we are forever con-
structing fictions from the truth. Not lies, but fictions. The world
surrounding us may be full of eternal truths and constitute an
everlasting real, but the world that we live within is an assem-
blage of data ordered by ourselves according to theories, stories,
habits, customs, and prejudices. We *make* sense. In making sense
of our environment we necessarily create a simulation of whatever it is that we are seeing, hearing, or reading (which can very
well be others' simulations).[31] It is not that reality doesn't exist—it
is more that by itself it doesn't really matter. Reality is always
refracted through the imagination, and it is through our imagination that we live our lives.

This does *not* mean that there is no such thing as truth. Truth
with a capital T may be an Enlightenment fantasy (one ironically

shared by religious fundamentalists), but there are standards of evidence upon which we can judge small "t" truths, accepting some as valid and rejecting others as invalid. But the important thing, as any scientist will tell you, is making a convincing case. Take the recent debate about evolution as an example. The creationists are correct in one thing at least: evolution is not the Truth; it is a theory.[32] But it is a good theory with a preponderance of evidence supporting it. "Intelligent design," the latest stalking horse of the creationists, which holds that a supreme being has guided evolution, is a lousy theory with no evidence behind it. What intelligent design does have, however, is a good publicity campaign. A public opinion poll in 2005 reported that 60 percent of Americans put their faith in theories of creationism or intelligent design, while only 26 percent believe in the evolution of life through natural selection, with the remainder not knowing or caring.[33] One side has the evidence, the other the compelling narrative.[34]

Politics is also not science. There are no immutable laws of gravity determining the outcome of an election, nor empirically verifiable tests of what constitutes a good society. Political systems are human creations that are then evaluated subjectively. As such, it is largely the power of public opinion that determines their form and value. This is something conservatives seem to understand better than progressives. The Brookings Institution, a liberal think tank, spends 3 percent of its budget on communications. The conservative Heritage Foundation, on the other hand, devotes 20 percent to what former vice president of communications Herb Berkowitz describes as "the selling of ideas." Berkowitz elaborates: "Our belief is that when the research product has been printed, then the job is only half done. That is when we start marketing it to the media. . . . We are actively out there selling these things, day after day. It's our mission."[35]

For years progressives have comforted themselves with age-old biblical adages that the "truth will out" or "the truth shall make you free," but waiting around for the truth to set you free is lazy politics.[36] The truth does not reveal itself by virtue of being the truth: it must be told, and we need to learn how to tell the truth more effectively. It must have stories woven around it, works of art made about it; it must be communicated in new ways and marketed so that it sells. It must be embedded in an experience that connects with people's dreams and desires, that resonates with the symbols and myths they find meaningful. The argument here is not for a progressive movement that lies outright, but rather for a propaganda of the truth. As William James once wrote: "Truth *happens* to an idea."[37]

Embracing dreams and making peace with spectacle does not necessarily mean abandoning a faith in the Enlightenment and empiricism, only acknowledging it is only that: a faith. Perhaps people can study—"judiciously, as you will"—the reality of the world and then make reasoned judgments that lead to political decisions and actions, but this is a way of seeing and being in the world that cannot have any taken-for-granted epistemological foundation. It is, to use postmodern cant, a system of discourse that must be (re)created, imagined, operationalized, and dramatized to appeal to the public's imagination.

While progressives are historically wedded to reason and reality, empiricism and the Enlightenment, there is a counterhistory of the left that has long embraced the dreamscape of the imaginary, using symbolism and narrative in an attempt to create new realities. One can cycle back through time to find examples: the story of Exodus symbolically transforming the Jews from slavery and servitude to the chosen people of God, or the miracles of Jesus giving hope to the poorest of the poor. In more modern times, one could consider the French Revolution, idealized in the name of reason and rationality but fought out on the streets in a swirl of competing fantasies. Examples closer to home might include the imagery of the Farm Security and Work Projects Administrations during the New Deal that gave form to a new vision of "the people," and Franklin Delano Roosevelt's intimate yet informative fireside chats that suggested a new understanding of citizens' relationship to political knowledge. Two decades later the ideal of reaching the promised land was transported from ancient Palestine to the black churches of the American South, animating the struggles for civil rights.

Consider the story of Rosa Parks. She is an ordinary woman who acts spontaneously from her own heart and changes the world. She is the Everywoman who hits that very American "I'm not going to take it anymore" breaking point. It is a moment of magical transformation, the "No!" that also becomes a "Yes!" affirming her dignity and humanity—and ours. It is also, as any serious student of the civil rights movement knows, a fiction, a deliberately perpetuated mythology. Rosa Parks may have been tired and wanting a seat, but she was not acting impulsively. She was a professional organizer, a secretary of the local chapter of the NAACP trained at the progressive Highlander Institute, who acted with a full understanding of the political ramifications of what she was doing. But what's more important, the history lesson or the myth?

Abbie Hoffman—the Yippie activist who dropped dollar bills on the stock exchange floor to create a miniriot of avarice and led 30,000 hippies in a mock-serious attempt to encircle and levitate the Pentagon—pursued an explicit strategy of mythmaking. Here he is explaining the logistics of organizing the protests that rocked the 1968 Democratic Party convention:

> We are faced with this task of getting huge numbers of people to
> come to Chicago along with hundreds of performers, artists, theater
> groups, engineers. Essentially, people involved in trying to work out
> a new society. How do you do this starting from scratch, with no or-
> ganization, no money, nothing? Well, the answer is that you create a
> myth. Something that people can play a role in, relate to.[38]

Hoffman understood how the game is played and made no apologies in his advice to fellow activists.

Look at Michael Moore. In his film *Bowling for Columbine*, does he
really lay out a rational, reasoned argument explaining the culture
of violence in the United States? No. Does seeing Charlton Heston
squirm under Moore's questioning bring us closer to the truth?
No. But was that scene an emotionally powerful argument for gun
control? Did the film put the issue on the table? Did it provoke
millions of Americans to give serious thought to the culture of
violence in America? Yes. Yes. And yes. Moore followed up on this
successful narrative formula in *Fahrenheit 9/11*. Contrary to what
conservative—and some liberal—critics have claimed, Moore isn't
simply telling tall tales.[39] But through clever editing, heartfelt in-
terviews, humorous stunts, and the insertion of himself into the
film, he is telling *a* tale. Folding facts into an enraging, touching,
funny, and personal narrative, Moore produced the most profitable "documentary" ever made.

Over the past few decades it has been activist groups to the far
left who have taken on the mantle of imagination. Anticorporate
globalization protesters in North America and Europe have eschewed the traditional model of mass protests in favor of a more
spectacular form. The old model of protest was simple and staid:
march, chant, and listen (to the truth from the leaders). The new
protests look nothing like this. With environmental protesters

dressed in sea turtle costumes in Seattle, theatrical skits involv-
ing the militant jesters of the Clandestine Insurgent Rebel Clown
Army in London and New York, or Ya Basta! in their padded *tutti
bianchi* (white jumpsuits) in Prague and Genoa, these protests are
infected with a general spirit of spirited anarchy. Declaring that
means are as important as ends (if not sometimes troublingly
more so), these mass protests create temporary autonomous
zones: a living, breathing, dancing imaginary form of a world
turned upside down. It's more than telling that the organizers
of the demonstration that shut down the City of London in 1998
called their protest a "Carnival Against Capitalism."

Further south, a man known only as Subcomandante Marcos,
whose poetic speeches and whimsical, fable-laced communiqués
weave a web of fantasy around the Zapatista rebellion in southern Mexico, recognizes that his comrades' black ski masks and
automatic weapons, far more than providing actual security or
a means of attack, are most effective as elements in a spectacle of resistance.[40] While to the east, in the Naramada Valley of
India, antidam activists hold educational puppet shows, symbolically drown a dam demon, and pledge civil disobedience, drawing
upon their local culture and traditions to create dramatic protests
against the state's plans to flood their land.[41]

Ironically, progressives once had a near monopoly on political
fantasy. Again, it was conservatives who wanted to defend the real
and retain the status quo, while radicals wanted to move toward
an imaginary future. After all, who is remembered for "I have a
dream"? But now, plagued by their Enlightenment guilt complex,
progressives regularly disown their own, often effective, history of
mobilizing fantasy, declaring that spectacle is silly, and that their
sense of superior seriousness will win debates, convince the public, and lead them back into the halls of power. Worse, spectacle

is what the *other* side does; a recent *New York Times* article listed one of the core qualities of Fascism as an "appeal to emotion and myth instead of reason."[42]

Examples of spectacular dissent are not hard to find. But when not rejected outright they are too often marginalized, understood as merely a tactic and not an integral way of thinking about and acting out politics. Then it's back to the "real" work of politics: acting soberly in the name of self-evident reality. March, chant, and listen . . . or study, lobby, and regulate. "Everything is theatrical," says David Solnit, who, as a founder of the activist group Art and Revolution, had a key role in giving the protest that shut down the city of Seattle in 1999 its particular spectacular flair. But the problem, as Solnit explains, is that "traditional protest—the march, the rally, the chants—is just bad theater."[43]

To be sure, many of the examples of spectacular dissent I have cited, and will describe in the pages to come, are marginal. Ironically, however, it may be political groups on the fringes that best appreciate and understand the mainstreams of culture in this country. Outsiders often have a clearer vision of the center than those deep within it, and for years these activists have been using their vantage point to observe how fantasy and spectacle are used by spinmeisters and marketers before trying such tactics themselves. For the most part the campaigns these activists wage and the demonstrations they stage engage hundreds, thousands, or tens of thousands of people, rather than millions or billions. But the potential for a spectacular politics is far greater, for everyday fantasy is employed effectively by the mass entertainment industry, and everyday spectacles *are* enthusiastically embraced by a majority of the world's population. The task at hand is to tap into this wide appeal and use it to build a truly popular progressive politics.

Perhaps the most important reason for progressives to make their peace with the politics of dreaming has little to do with the immediate task of winning consent or creating dissent, but has instead to do with long-term vision. Without dreams we will never be able to imagine the new world we want to build. From the 1930s until the 1980s political conservatives in this country were lost: out of power and out of touch. Recalling those days, Karl Rove, George W. Bush's senior political adviser, says: "We were relegated to the desert."[44] While many a pragmatic Republican moved to the center, a critical core kept wandering in that desert, hallucinating a political world considered fantastic by postwar standards: a preemptive military, radical tax cuts, eroding the line between church and state, ending welfare, and privatizing Social Security. Look where their dreams are today.

As I write these words, the right's phantasmagoria seems to be crumbling. Forced into a courtroom in Dover, Pennsylvania, the proponents of "intelligent design" acted out the part of mendacious fools on a public stage.[45] The story of stories that Christianity should be equated with the Republican Party is being rewritten as evangelicals in recent months have taken on "liberal" issues like the environment, poverty, and AIDS.[46] Revelations of manufactured evidence of weapons of mass destruction continue to reveal the cynical machinations of fantasy construction, and the bungling of the war in Iraq and the response to Hurricane Katrina have eroded the myth of the competency of Bush's CEO presidency. When centrist politicians like ex-Marine-now-Democratic-representative John Murtha publicly declare the war they once supported "a flawed policy wrapped in an illusion," it is tempting to believe that progressives were right all along.[47] Truth will out after all; stay the course and all will be fine. But this would be a miscalculation. The terrain of politics has irrevocably shifted.

False fantasies may have been revealed, but the dreams that animate them live on.

Progressives are at a crossroads. To continue straight on, confident of the inalienability of "Enlightenment principles and empiricism," is to cloak ourselves in the irrelevancies of the past. It is a safe journey, for even nightmares, as long as they are familiar, offer the solace of the known. But this journey leads nowhere. The rationality and reason that once freed us from authority now make us equivocating cowards, judiciously studying reality instead of changing it. The other way—to create reality using unfamiliar tools—is to take a leap into the unknown. This way is not secure: the leap can lead to the exuberance of the French Terror, the mass ecstasy of Nazi rallies, the apocalyptic dreams of jihad, or even the monstrous banality of Andrew Lloyd Weber's latest hit musical.

Theories (and theorists) of the politics of spectacle and fantasy have steered people to some pretty unsavory places. Gustav LeBon's observations on the irrational behavior of crowds was appreciated and applied by Adolf Hitler and Joseph Goebbels, as well as public relations pioneer Edward Bernays. Friedrich Nietzsche's philosophy of will was appropriated by the Nazis. Georges Sorel's mobilizing "myth of the general strike" led him toward Fascism. And Walter Lippmann came to reject popular democracy as unworkable, characterizing the citizenry as a "bewildered herd" who, blinded by symbols and stereotypes, were best relegated to being merely "spectators of action."[48] I, however, do not think that recognizing the power of a politics past reason means a sure slide toward Fascism (or a career as a creative director on Madison Avenue). To clear another path we need to separate what has happened from what could happen.

First, we need to survey the terrain of today's imagination. We need to take apart the current manifestations of dreams, study contemporary spectacles, and understand how the modern manufacturers of consent channel these dynamics. Then we can begin to imagine how popular desires might be expressed in other ways and via different vehicles.

Progressives like to study and to know. We like to be right (and then complain that others are not). But being right is not enough—we need to win. And to win we need to act. What follows are observations and suggestions that might guide our actions. I'm inviting readers, wherever they might fall on the progressive political spectrum, from pragmatic liberals to utopian anarchists, street activists to pissed-off voters, to join me in imagining a way of moving our dreams into reality. In these pages I do not lay out an ideological line to follow, nor will I prescribe policies to enact. Instead, this book offers up an alternative political aesthetic for progressives to consider; a theory of *dreampolitik* they might practice. Some of the political examples I use in the following pages may seem particular, and perhaps a bit peculiar. They are largely drawn from my activist experience on the far left, and the particular—and perhaps a bit peculiar—political scene of lower Manhattan. But there is no reason why this way of thinking and doing cannot be adopted and adapted by progressives who live in different places, come from different traditions, and have different personalities. Their practice of *dreampolitik* will look different—it should. This endeavor involves taking risks. There is also no guarantee that this strategy will work, no Enlightenment assurance that this is the one true way. To embrace dreams as part of a winning strategy for progressive politics may be just a dream itself, but really, at this point, what do we have to lose?

2. Learn from Las Vegas:
Spectacular Vernacular
with Andrew Boyd

The S-3B Viking Navy jet screams down onto the flight deck of the USS *Abraham Lincoln*. Its extended tailhook catches the carrier's steel cable and two g's of force bear down upon the president of the United States, bringing the plane to a standstill in a mere 350 feet. In full flight suit, his crotch bulging subtly, the president steps out of the four-seat fighter-bomber to cheering throngs of servicemen returning from the Iraq war. He gives them a thrilling thumbs-up sign. The media is enraptured. "History in the making," says one cable news commentator. "Spectacular," another claims, astutely.[1] After changing out of the flight jacket into a suit and tie, the president addresses the five thousand sailors standing in impressive, uniform-white rows on the carrier deck, announcing the "end of major combat operations in Iraq" while a huge red, white, and blue banner proclaiming "Mission Accomplished" waves above.

Progressives know all this was a lie. We eagerly point out to the few who will listen that President Bush avoided declaring a literal "victory" to circumvent legal repercussions under the Geneva

Convention. We explain that the enlistees onboard the carrier were bound by military discipline to applaud him. We describe how the podium was aligned so the TV crews would have the S-3B Viking in the background of the shot with the "Mission Accomplished" banner draped across the bridge above it. We tell people that the carrier itself, already held at sea and delaying the homecoming of servicemen returning from an unprecedented ten-month tour of duty, was angled to obscure a view of the coastline only thirty-seven miles away. We report that normally a carrier would need to be at least two hundred miles out to sea to require the use of the fighter-bomber rather than the usual Marine One helicopter. We know, in brief, that the whole affair was a manufactured spectacle.

We shake our heads in shame and disbelief at the seeming gullibility of our countrymen and countrywomen as we see the real history of the president's less-than-heroic performance in the Texas Air National Guard during the Vietnam War dissolve in a carefully stagecrafted series of associations of our president with military prowess. As we watch the facts and complexities of the Iraq war, as well as the larger and darker political machinations behind it, become subsumed by mythic imagery, scenes from *Triumph of the Will*, Leni Riefenstahl's filmic celebration of the 1934 Nazi Party rally, haunt our imagination.

Why do we have such a virulent reaction to this political stagecraft? Certainly, we're upset by the hypocrisy and shameless triumphalism of a political adversary. And yes, progressives are creatures of the Enlightenment with an abiding faith in reason and reality. But there is something more to this, something deeper. We are afraid of the spectacle.

What is spectacle? By default most people think of throwing Christians to the lions, parading missiles through Red Square, or maybe the Ice Capades. But spectacle is something more. It is a way of making an argument. Not through appeals to reason, rationality, and self-evident truth, but instead through story and myth, fears and desire, imagination and fantasy. It realizes what reality cannot represent. It is the animation of an abstraction, a transformation from ideal to expression. *Spectacle is a dream on display.*

Spectacle has a long history in politics, stretching back to the Circus Maximus of imperial Rome and likely long before. But it takes on new importance in the age of popular democracy. In a democracy, leaders not only need to keep the masses from running riot in the street but, more important, they need their consent to govern. Progressives are quite adept at the critique of this "manufacture of consent," but we need to learn how to construct dissent—and consent—as well. We need to acknowledge that politics—even our own politics—is about persuasion, and that one of the most effective ways to persuade people, and effect change, is to tap into their dreams. If progressives are going to take politics and power seriously, we need to learn to use spectacle not grudgingly but enthusiastically and free of guilt. We need to make spectacle our own.

But what, then, separates our spectacle from theirs? Do our recognition and embrace of the nonrational lead inexorably to a relativistic "battle of the myths"? Does the manufacture of consent, or dissent, necessitate ignorance and blind obedience? No. There is the possibility that spectacle can honor progressive ideals. Ironically, it is Las Vegas—Sin City itself—that might help us begin to formulate such an ethical spectacle. Among the whimsical, over-the-top, crassly commercial simulations of Vegas lies a model of spectacle that is more populist and more participatory— yet maybe no less effective—than Bush's landing on the USS *Lincoln.* Progressives have a lot to learn from Las Vegas.

In the early 1970s three East Coast establishment architects visited Las Vegas. Out there in the Nevada desert, Robert Venturi, Denise Scott Brown, and Steven Izenour found an antidote to the European architectural modernism of gray poured-concrete towers and sterile glass blocks. With its billboards, neon signs, garish casinos, and vast parking lots, Las Vegas was an architecture of bold communication and commercial persuasion which scorched the cool theories of respectable design. Whereas modernism whispered the structural truth of buildings with its stripped-down architecture and exposed materials, the gaudy style of the Vegas Strip screamed out unlikely but alluring promises: Golden Nugget, Stardust, Mirage, and then, as it stretched into the desert, "Quick Cash Here" and "Girls, Girls, Girls."

In 1972, Venturi, Brown, and Izenour wrote a manifesto celebrating the vernacular of the roadside called *Learning from Las Vegas*. What is remembered about *Learning from Las Vegas* today is the architects' celebration of historical pastiche and eclectic style: the way that the casinos on the Strip mixed Egyptian with Baroque, Classical with Arabesque. The book launched an anti-theory of architecture which, predictably, became the field's new reigning theory. In graduate schools, *Learning from Las Vegas* is still read as one of the founding texts of aesthetic postmodernism.

But in 1972, the lessons Venturi, Brown, and Izenour seemed most eager to impart had more to do with hubris and humility. It wasn't so much that the architects loved Las Vegas, but they loved the fact that so many people loved Las Vegas (6.8 million visited in 1970).[2] Since the architects' job was to build spaces for people to inhabit, they reasoned that it was important to pay attention to popular style. If people liked garish display, improbable historical juxtapositions, and convenient parking—signs and surfaces rather than boldness of pure form and integrity of the material—

who were architects to deny this? "As Experts with Ideals," they wrote, modern architects too often "build for Man rather than for people."[3] The authors wanted to reverse this, paying attention to people's values and then designing buildings utilizing the popular vernacular. Their argument was not that the customer is always right; it was a rejection of the notion that people's desires are always wrong. The ideal was not to capitulate, but to *learn* from Las Vegas.

What does a book on architecture have to do with politics? A lot. Progressives tend to think about politics in terms of ideals. This is good—without ideals we would have nothing to fight for. The problem is that these ideals are too frequently divorced from the dreams of the rest of the population. In a dictatorship this doesn't pose a problem. As "Experts with Ideals," we could merely impose our vision on everyone else. But in a democracy this simply won't do. That *everyone* has a say in governance is the fundamental principle of democracy; that you cannot govern without the consent and support of the people is central to its practice. Ethically and practically, progressives need to understand popular dreams. If the masses like Las Vegas, then progressives have got to figure out what it is about Las Vegas they like.

"The deepest error of our political thinking [is] to talk of politics without reference to human beings," wrote Walter Lippmann in his first book, *A Preface to Politics*.[4] Oddly enough, it might be the very same man who coined the term "the manufacture of consent" and ended up rejecting democracy as unworkable who can help progressives learn what Las Vegas has to teach us about a popular and passionate democracy. Lippmann was once a progressive himself. He formed the Socialist Club as an undergraduate at Harvard, worked as a researcher for the great muckraker Lincoln Steffens upon graduation, and held a job in the administration of

the socialist mayor of Schenectady, New York.[5] In these positions
Lippmann noticed something. The rational appeals of reformers
often fell upon deaf ears. Successful politicians—like those of the
great, and greatly corrupt, urban political machines—spoke to the
heart as much as to the head. Progressives spoke to abstract Man
while organizations like New York City's infamous Tammany Hall
appealed to real people.

Lippmann's evolving theories about what motivated human
beings and what that meant for the practice of politics were influenced by ideas swirling around him. He had struck up a relationship with William James while at college and was inspired by
his ideas about the "moral equivalent of war." Lippmann also developed a friendship with Graham Wallas, a British socialist who
stressed the political importance of understanding the irrational.
And finally, he, like most intellectuals of his time, was just beginning to comprehend the radical new theories of Sigmund Freud.
Indeed, during the summer Lippmann spent writing A *Preface to
Politics* in the backwoods of Maine, his cabin mate was working on
translating Freud into English.

Lippmann borrows two ideas from Freud, altering them to
meet his needs. The first was the concept of *taboo*. Taboos are re-
strictions, prohibitive laws laid down by society to ensure stability.
For Freud, the root taboo was on incest, revealing itself in ancient
Greek stories like that of Oedipus, a young man fated to kill his
father and bed his mother. Lippmann uses taboo more liberally,
defining it politically as the impulse to "abolish human instincts"
in the effort to bring about social change.[6] Reformers often ruled
by taboo, legislating against popular desires such as drinking,
gambling, and promiscuous sex. The primary taboo of progressives, however, is on allowing the irrational to play a positive role
in politics. Then, as now, the progressive MO was to be practical,

consider all the ramifications, and then create a committee to make recommendations. Judicious study is always what's called for. Lippmann was all for study but believed that the myopic search for the rational solution to social problems often missed the point. "For human nature seems to have wants that must be filled," he argued. "The demand for pleasure, adventure, romance has been left to the devil's catering for so long a time that most people think that he inspires demand. He doesn't."[7]

We do. We are the ones who demand pleasure, adventure, and romance. Understanding this, Lippmann's theory of politics represents a radical—or, at first glance, conservative—acceptance of who humans are and what they desire.[8] Like the modernist architects that Venturi and his colleagues criticized, progressives are all too fond of fashioning solutions that depend upon an idealized model of humanity to work. They imagine Man as he could be: sober, reasoning, and upstanding—not men and women as they are: emotional, passionate, and prone to fits of fantasy. And if people don't play the part progressives have written for them, then it is the progressive's job to step in and keep them from their evil ways. Taboo.

Those of us left-of-center today like to think that taboo is now the property of conservatives. It was Nancy Reagan, after all, who made "Just Say No" the Republican Party's response to drug use. We, on the other hand, are neither Nancy Reagan Republicans nor the Prohibitionist Progressives of Lippmann's era, but the libertine children of the freewheeling sixties.[9] Certainly this is how conservatives now think of us. But taboo is still very much in operation in liberal politics; it is just no longer focused on loose women, games of chance, and devil water. Think of how progressives often frame their demands for ending dependence on fossil fuels: don't buy a sport utility vehicle, don't drive over 55 miles per hour,

don't waste gas. Don't, don't, don't. We witnessed the epitome
of this politics of liberal taboo when President Jimmy Carter appeared on national television in 1977 to talk about the energy crisis. Wearing a cardigan sweater, he told Americans to turn down
their thermostats and stop being so selfish. Carter may have been
correct, but he was also widely ridiculed and resented, and his
one term in office was followed by eight years of gas-guzzling policies implemented by his successor, Ronald Reagan.

It's fun to drive fast, one feels feel invincible in an SUV, and bare
skin is sexy. This doesn't mean that wasting energy should be celebrated, only that it is worth figuring out why people do it before
simply condemning, regulating, and repressing. Acknowledging
the present passions of people is not the same thing as accepting
things as they are. Instead, current desire is the fulcrum on which
to leverage future change. As Lippmann argues, "Instead of taboo-
ing our impulses, we must redirect them."[10]

This is where he borrows another concept from Freud: *sublimation*. Sublimation is as necessary for civilization as taboo—but
much more effective. Whereas the taboo is the restriction of a
harmful impulse, sublimation is its redirection. For Freud the
primary impulse was the sex drive, *eros*, to which he later added
thanatos, or destruction. Left to our libidinal impulses we humans
would destroy one another, screwing and killing like an apocalyptic episode of Marlin Perkins's *Wild Kingdom*. We don't do this (or
at least most of us don't) because we've learned to channel these
nihilistic impulses into safer ends: insatiable sex becomes loving
relationships, ceaseless destruction is expressed through shoot-
'em-up video games like *Grand Theft Auto*.

As he did with taboo, Lippmann broadened Freud's concept of
sublimation and expanded its application. The solution to social
problems like "vice" was not repression but a political response

that recognized the impulses that feed vice and then channeled such desires into more socially desirable outlets like dance halls and social recreation.[11] But more important, Lippmann recognized that sublimation needn't merely apply to the redirection of problematic human drives; it could be used to think more widely about creating a politics that was responsive to human beings in *all* their desires. "No genuine politician ever treats his constituents as reasoning animals," Lippmann writes in a passage worth quoting at length:

> This is as true of the high politics of Isaiah as it is of the ward boss. Only the pathetic amateur deludes himself into thinking that, if he presents the major and minor premises, the voter will automatically draw the conclusion on election day. The successful politician— good and bad—deals with the dynamics—with the will, the hopes, the needs and the visions of men.[12]

This last line is important, for with it Lippmann opens up the idea of sublimation. The traditional psychoanalytic definition of sublimation assumes that human desires are destructive: rapacious sexuality and a violence unto death. But Lippmann, in arguing for the political direction of human desires, includes "dynamics" far more noble: people's hopes and visions. The irrational and the emotional are not intrinsically negative aspects of politics. They are not something that must be prohibited, nor even necessarily something that must be civilized; they can be noble and good.[13] They are, however, something that needs to be addressed if one hopes to attain, and hold, political power.

So what sort of deal does a savvy politician strike with the often irrational dynamics of his or her constituents? The first is to recognize that current manifestations are not indicative of future possibilities. "It is probably true that the impulses of man have changed very little within recorded history," Lippmann writes. "What has changed enormously from epoch to epoch is the character in which these impulses appear."[14] Men and women, for example, have likely felt what we now call romantic love since the beginning of time, but the idea that one would consummate that love with the person one marries, or even with someone of the opposite sex, is merely its present character. Arranged marriages and same-sex romantic relationships among the classical Greeks were another such manifestation. What remains constant is the emotionally charged dynamic.

Americans' current desires for security often manifest themselves in fantasies of safety within gated communities and SUVs, and their fears are answered by the continuing spectacle of the War on Terror. The theory Lippmann presents to us suggests that we acknowledge the enduring desire to be safe but also ask ourselves whether there are other ways in which this dynamic can be expressed and addressed. Could security come from more stable communities? Could more stable communities come from feeling more secure in our health, work, education, and housing? Progressives can come up with better solutions to address people's desire for security than gated communities, SUVs, and eroding civil liberties, but only if we start from the right place: acknowledging these root desires.

Recognizing and working with popular desire makes sense from a pragmatic point of view, but taking dreams seriously opens up possibility on a more theoretical level as well, for it reverses the relationship between political reason and desire as it has been commonly theorized since Aristotle. Reason has traditionally been used as a club with which to beat desire into submission. Political theorists excise it, reformers prohibit it. Instead, I would argue, the function of rationality is to give form, shape, and concrete expression to irrational dreams. To be effective in the world, to change the world, progressives ought, in the heady words of the young Walter Lippmann, "make reason serve the irrational."[15]

A recent progressive attempt to understand popular hopes and visions and give political substance to some of these ephemeral dynamics is the Apollo Project. Organized in the spring of 2003 by two progressive think tanks, the Institute for America's Future and the Center on Wisconsin Strategy, Apollo is an alliance of heavy hitters from U.S. environmental and union movements. Apollo promotes fairly traditional progressive environmental policies: public investment in sustainable energy sources and energy conservation through infrastructural development. What's novel is how the project packages and sells these policies. Their choice of name tips off their strategy. By bundling their policies under the name Apollo, and through conscious—and constant—comparisons with President Kennedy's 1961 space initiative, they hope to harness some of the optimism and patriotism (and funding) attached to the moon landing. Acting executive director Jeff Rickert explains that Apollo is more than a name. It's "a metaphor" which "sparks imagination."[16] Rickert's hope is that evoking the moon shot of 1961 will remind Americans that they once found common cause in a peaceful national project, and can do so again.

Apollo addresses multiple desires simultaneously: the environmentalist's dream of smog-free air, the patriot's longing for national autonomy and independence, and the blue-collar worker's hope for U.S.-based jobs. "Clean energy. A safer world. Jobs with a future" is the sound bite repeated by Apollo advocate and former Clinton administration chief of staff John Podesta.[17] As Rickert explains, the project is about "changing the frame of the debate in order to broaden the coalition" by "removing the wedges" of jobs vs. environment and global warming vs. national interest that have been used to divide constituencies. Apollo, then, provides a new—and inclusive—symbol that redirects these potentially divisive desires toward a common material goal: national sustainable energy.[18]

By drawing from and then speaking to a wide range of citizens' fantasies (or at least political, labor, and environmental leaders' fantasies of their constituents' fantasies) Apollo has assembled a notable list of supporters, including twenty-three labor unions, twenty-five state and local labor councils, most major environmental groups, and an impressive number of community organizations, liberal politicians, and progressive business leaders. More important, Apollo has been able to translate this ideal into local success on the ground. Through the work of more than a hundred community groups, and backed by the muscle of organized labor, Apollo pressured the state of Washington to pass a green building code that sets environmental standards for all new public buildings. Pennsylvania—a coal state, no less—has adopted an alternative energy bill that mandates clean energy standards. And California has committed to investing more than $400 million from the public employee and public teachers' retirement fund in the clean-energy sector. Still far from their goal of a national funding initiative on the level of the space program, it is an impressive start for an organization only a few years old.[19]

The Apollo Project is a smart, savvy, strategic effort to listen to, respect, and address "the will, the hopes, the needs and the visions of men," as Lippmann put it, and then frame progressive policies in such a way as to speak back to these "dynamics." Apollo rather blandly calls this "a positive strategy" on its official Web site.[20] A more accurate description of the project comes from Michael Shellenberger, a founder of the organization. Apollo, he says approvingly, is "a dream."[21]

Progressives could benefit by studying dreams more diligently. Fortunately, we have a ready-made laboratory at our disposal. Unfortunately, it takes the form of something progressives traditionally disdain: commercial culture. To be sure, there are disadvantages to living in a consumer society like that in the United States, where the success of culture is measured in how well it sells. Mass appeal does not necessarily result in the "the best which has been thought and said in the world," to quote Matthew Arnold's classic definition of culture. And defining the "public interest" as what interests the mass public has serious ramifications in terms of providing the quality information necessary for an informed citizenry.[22] But for our purposes here, there are real advantages to a market-driven culture.

When the British Broadcasting Corporation funds the television dramatization of a nineteenth-century novel, the popularity of the program is only one of their concerns. What matters as much, if not more, is whether the programming appeals to their own elite Oxbridge sensibility and their ideal of an educated public. This is not the case in the United States (and increasingly less so in Britain, too). Here one can be sure that if a program is on TV for more than a season, if a play is staged and runs for more than a week, or if an album climbs the charts, it is appealing to a paying population. In the long run, no amount of studio promotion, disc jockey payola, or ideological interest overrides the logic of the market. If culture stays, and sells, it means that it somehow resonates with the popular will. And anyone interested in democratic politics ignores such enthusiasm at his or her peril.

This does not necessitate some sort of pseudopopulist embrace of the entirety of popular culture (we needn't contort ourselves to reclaim *Cats*). But it does mean that we need to recognize that in these expressions some popular will is being expressed. *How* that will is being manifested in popular culture may be something to condemn—or applaud—but the will itself has to be dealt with. If it isn't, if it's ignored in our political platforms and policies, then all that energy of the people applauding on Broadway, watching *Survivor*, or listening to hit radio will remain static and then dissipate quietly (or be captured by others).

Lippmann didn't think much of popular culture. On the public's fascination with baseball scores, he had this to say: "Watch the crowds in front of a bulletin board, finding a vicarious excitement and an abstract relief from the monotony of their lives. What a second-hand civilization it is that grows passionate over a scorecard with little electric lights!"[23] But he understood that in order to understand the population, he needed to know what people saw while gazing up at those little lights. As he concludes, "Being lofty about the 'passing fad' and the ephemeral outcry is all very well in the biographies of dead men, but rank nonsense in the rulers of real ones."[24] Politicos don't need to think much of popular culture, but they do need to think a lot about it.

This is why it is worth thinking about Las Vegas. The city has transformed itself in the thirty years since Venturi, Brown, and Izenour visited. Casino ownership has moved from mobsters to the (aptly named) MGM-Mirage group, and the sleazy swinger style of the Rat Pack has given way to whole (if not entirely wholesome) family vacation packages. Its hotels and restaurants receive top ratings worldwide, and it is the center of some of the most dynamic union organizing in the nation. As of this writing Las Vegas is the fastest growing city in the United States. But perhaps the most noticeable transformation has been that of the architecture, or "architainment" as *Nation* writer Marc Cooper calls it.[25] Cheap billboards, garish neon, and blocky casinos have been usurped by an elaborate faux New York skyline, or immediately recognizable, if oddly positioned, landmarks of Paris. Down the street are Egyptian pyramids made of glass, and up the Strip lie the grand palaces of a virtual Venice.[26] The fantasy and fakery that was always a part of Vegas in places like Caesar's Palace and Circus, Circus has been taking steroids since 1972.

It is the nature of this fantasy and fakery that is so interesting. It's so obvious. Yes, Las Vegas is fake. This is decried by sober American thinkers (the evisceration of reality by its simulation) and celebrated by enthusiastic French intellectuals (the evisceration of reality by its simulation!) but both seem to miss the point. A fake is only fake if people believe that it references a "real." It's doubtful that anyone mistakes New York, New York for the real thing or, having visited the Great Pyramid of Luxor, feels they've gone to Egypt. The crowds that love Las Vegas know that it is fake, and that's part of the reason they love it.

Contemporary Las Vegas symbolizes a different type of spectacle than those manufactured by Leni Riefenstahl or the directors of *George W. Bush: The Movie*. The latter hope to pass themselves off as real; the former's very appeal lies in its patent falsity. People enjoy Las Vegas because they know it is just a spectacle. The sights of Paris, across the street from Venice, and down the block from the Brooklyn Bridge. How exciting! The appeal of Las Vegas is not based in trickery (other than the odds at the gambling tables); the Strip is a transparent spectacle. *What is being sold, and what is being enjoyed, is illusion—but not delusion.*

Las Vegas is not the first, nor only, cultural form to parade its artificiality. The nineteenth-century French poet Charles Baudelaire, in a dig at the Enlightenment celebration of the nobility of nature, praised the use of cosmetics by women. His admiration was not

for makeup that accentuated a woman's natural beauty, but for
the garish display of artificiality that allowed her to transcend nature and become a self-conscious work of art.[27] A century later, the
critic Susan Sontag argued that the signature characteristic of the
cultural sensibility known as "camp" is "its love of the unnatural:
of artifice and exaggeration." The over-the-top performances of
Joan Crawford in *Mildred Pierce* or Bette Davis in *All About Eve* work
as camp because they are recognized and appreciated as over the
top: "Being-as-Playing-a-Role," as Sontag describes it.[28] Set against
a modern cultural tradition which celebrates the authentic expression of the true self, camp revels in the obviously inauthentic.
In our new century the popularity of the staged spectacle of professional wrestling perhaps best exhibits the perseverance of the
desire to enjoy a fantasy that one knows is just a fantasy.

What would a self-conscious, transparent spectacle translated
into progressive politics look like? It's hard to say, but there's a
recent campaign that gives a hint.

"Yes, I'm a Billionaire. And, yes, I'm for Bush," says the earnest young man to the Fox News reporter. Enjoying the crisp New
Hampshire autumn at a protest "against" presidential candidate
Howard Dean, the young man—impeccably dressed in a double-
breasted suit, bowler hat, walking stick, and monocle—certainly
looks like a billionaire, or at least like someone trying to look like
someone trying to look like a billionaire. Protesting against the
Democratic candidates and popping champagne corks at Bush
campaign stops, such characters were commonplace during the
2004 election. It's was all part of a satirical media campaign called
"Billionaires for Bush."

The "Billionaires" campaign began its life as Billionaires for
Bush (or Gore) during the 2000 election when anticorporate direct
action activists banded together with more mainstream campaign

finance advocates to challenge what they perceived to be the corruption of both political parties by big money. In 2004, after four
years in which the Democrats were relegated to a weak minor-
ity party and the Bush administration became exhibit A of crony-
capitalism and corporate pandering, the campaign was reborn as
simply Billionaires for Bush.

Within the conservative common sense of contemporary
politics, straight-on arguments for greater economic fairness
are regularly framed and then dismissed as "class warfare." The
Billionaires for Bush, by camping it up as the super-wealthy and
cheering on George Bush and his economic policies, used humor
to sidestep this frame while still painting the president as a friend
of the corporate elite. It was a backdoor strategy allowing activists
to show—in surprisingly sharp terms—who were the economic
winners and losers of the Bush administration's policies. Marxism,
Groucho-style.

While checking its facts carefully and closely collaborating
with more serious economic justice groups like United for a Fair
Economy, the campaign borrowed heavily from the mythmak-
ers of Madison Avenue. With high production values, a branding
campaign built around its name and logo (a red, white, and
blue piggy bank), and a viral promotion strategy that invited in-
character participation, the campaign grew from one to one hundred chapters in a few months, built a 10,000-member e-mail list,
put on six nationwide days of action and countless local ones, and
garnered attention from more than 250 mainstream media
outlets.[29]

One of the early actions that put the Billionaires on the media
map occurred during a 2004 fund-raiser for "Bush's Brain," Karl
Rove. As Billionaire founder Andrew Boyd describes it:

In February we got wind that Rove was coming to New York for a fund-raising dinner. Twenty of us assembled in a nearby park, dressed in tuxedos, top hats, gowns, and tiaras, and marched toward the club, chanting "Karl Rove is innocent! Karl Rove is innocent!"

People stopped to look, and behind their curious faces, you could almost hear the mental gears clicking: "Innocent? . . . hmmm . . . so, wait . . . what's he not guilty of?" We had a long list of all that he was "not guilty of" (push-polling, misinformation, political dirty tricks, etc.) laid out in a leaflet, which we handed them.

When we reached the club where the fund-raiser was being held some protesters from the Sierra Club were already there. You could tell they were protesters because, unlike us, they didn't have matching outfits, and their signs were hand-scrawled, unlike our perfectly lettered placards. You could also tell they were protesters because the NYPD had stuck them in a protest pen on the other side of the street.

Where did they put us? Right in front of the club, right next to all these buttoned-down Wall Street execs lined up waiting to get inside. We turned to them and chanted, "Write big checks!" Then we turned to face the Sierra Club protesters and chanted, "Buy your own president!"

Eventually the police figured out who we really were and stuck us in the pens along with the poorly dressed Sierra Club protesters. But immediately after they'd done that, a black town car arrived. "It's Karl Rove," someone said. We began shouting "Karl Rove is innocent!" as he exited the car and strode up the steps of the club. He must have heard us, because he turned around and looked over at us. He saw our banner, "Billionaires for Bush—Government Of, By, and For the Corporations," and came over to shake hands with us.

The TV media crushed in to capture the scene. He turned to the cameras: "These are my supporters." The cops and the club's security were all freaking out. The Sierra Club folks even got into the act, shouting, "Shame! Shame!" right in the guy's face. In spite of this, he popped under the barricades and joined hands with us. Finally, with a big wink, he revealed himself to be Tony Torn, professional actor, stealth Billionaire, and, with the help of a little talcum powder, a pretty damn good Karl Rove impersonator.

Luckily, the *Times* was writing all this down, and their article the following day was picked up on the blogs and news portals. It became a word-of-mouth favorite, helping to insinuate the "Billionaires for Bush" virus into the hearts, minds, and funny bones of voters across the nation.[30]

During the 2004 presidential campaign the Billionaires rented a stretch limo, went on several "limo tours" through swing-state regions, and then held a "Million Billionaire March" during the Republican National Convention in which 400 Billionaires from over thirty states paraded down Fifth Avenue sporting banners and placards reading "Corporations Are People Too," "Free the Enron 7!" "Widen the Income Gap," "Privatize Everything," and "We Paid for 8 Years." After their candidate had won the election, the Billionaires initiated a preemptive Cheney Legal Defense Fund— just in case. On Labor Day they staged a "Cheap Labor Day," and on April 15, tax day, Billionaires accosted taxpayers on the steps of post offices in cities across the country with lines like "Thank you for paying more than your fair share" and "We couldn't have done it without you."

What is noteworthy about the whole spectacle of Billionaires for Bush, given its popularity with both participants and press, is that nobody was fooled, at least not for long. Everyone, maybe after some initial uncertainty, realized that these were not real billionaires but people playing at being billionaires: "Being-as-Playing-a-Role." This didn't stop people from enjoying themselves at campaign stops or fancy-dress fund-raising balls. Like the faux buildings of Las Vegas, the artificiality of the Billionaires didn't seem to detract from its enjoyment. And, as I argue in a later chapter, this patent artificiality made their message *more* effective in that it drew attention to the corresponding charade of a politics in the service of "people of wealth" which passes itself off as a democracy—that is: the Billionaires' charade highlights the falsity of our supposed reality.

Both the Billionaires and Las Vegas point to a novel way of creating and understanding spectacle. Spectacle in the employ of the Bush administration is about pretending to be real: the president is a real war hero, the war in Iraq has really been won. It is about distraction and substitution. The spectacle in the Nevada desert works according to different principles: spectacle that is understood as spectacle, one that still has symbolic power but lets the audience in on the production. And where the engineered fantasy of George Bush landing on the USS *Lincoln* has collapsed under the weight of its own falsity, and the president's popularity with the public seems to slip daily, the attractions of Las Vegas are going strong. In spite of gambling being legalized in other locales across the United States, the number of visitors to Vegas has increased 450 percent over the past thirty years. More than 37 million people visited Las Vegas in 2004, spending nearly $34 billion.[31] One can't discount the draw of old-fashioned, unsublimated desires (gambling and prostitution) in accounting for the success of Sin City. As the refreshingly frank advertising slogan of the Las Vegas Convention and Visitors Authority promises: "What happens here,

stays here." But one also shouldn't overlook the appeal of a spectacle that doesn't treat its audience like suckers. This is a lesson
that progressives might learn.

Admiration of Las Vegas has its limits. Las Vegas is a spectacle, no matter how transparent and self-conscious, whose function is to rejuvenate and replenish, not challenge, the current
system. Gambling is the myth of post-Calvinist capitalism at its
most extreme: with one lucky roll of the dice you can eradicate
inequality—your own, that is. And for the rest of the family the
spectacle is a respite, a vacation from a world increasingly complex and hostile. Scared to take an international flight because of
terrorists? Stay at the Italianate Bellagio instead, and while you're
there, cross the street to the Eiffel Tower, and then on to Egypt.
Don't worry about the state of the world—escape it.

In the shadows of Las Vegas's neon glow hides a regressive tax
structure and a shabby social service system. Nevada has the second highest potential tax revenue of all the states, yet the taxes it
collects are the third lowest in the country. With no general business or income tax, sales and consumer taxes, which hit the poor
the hardest, make up the gap—but not adequately. When it comes
to public education, the state spends $1,100 less per student than
Mississippi. Nevada is thirty-eighth in the nation in health services, and it is fifty-first in Medicaid spending (after Washington,
D.C.).[32] In the end, Las Vegas is a spectacle that hides its own tawdry reality. But on those garish, neon-saturated streets lies the
specter of another spectacle, one that could question, disinte-
grate, and reimagine the world in which we live. And, critically, it
is a spectacle which is popular with the public.

"We pin our hopes to the sporting public," Bertolt Brecht wrote
in 1926 in an essay directed to his fellow playwrights and directors who were bemoaning the fact that the masses preferred soc-

cer matches to serious theater. Instead of whining about the lack of taste of the masses, the radical dramaturge, like Lippmann before him, believed that you could learn something useful from sporting events, the primary lesson being that people participate in what they enjoy, and unless theater was made enjoyable, the people wouldn't come.

Many of Brecht's radical contemporaries were content to make theater, or derive theory, based upon the assumption that their good intentions and well-reasoned analysis were all that was required, and that the people, once suitably awakened, would find their truths self-evident. Brecht rejected this. He believed that to be effective as a playwright or a politico, one must embrace the present. He took the position of a (strategic) weathervane, testing the popular wind and fashioning a political theater that sailed with it. Like the authors of *Learning from Las Vegas*, Brecht was not suggesting a public-opinion-poll politics of giving the people whatever they want and then slavishly following in their wake. He understood that catching the wind did not dictate the direction that one traveled, because, in his words, "Once one has a wind one can naturally sail against it; the only impossibility is to sail with no wind at all or with tomorrow's wind."[33] Tragically, in Brecht's Germany, it was the Nazi Party that ended up being his best students.

Today it is the right in the United States which seems to be learning from Las Vegas. The stagecraft of the Bush administration has obfuscated an unprecedented redistribution of wealth and the launching of a new American empire with stories of Dubya's folksy Texas ranch and images of toppling statues in Iraq. Many progressives shake their heads at these sorry spectacles, consoling their impotence with a sense of moral superiority—"We would never fall for such a thing"—and hoping that some day the wind will blow back in the direction of the mythic republic of letters and reason of the eighteenth century. Today's wind is one of spectacle. It may not be of our making. Its origins may not be the pure lands of the Enlightenment but instead the commercial barrens of entertainment and the swamps of Fascism. But use it we must, for without the wind, we are becalmed, stuck, going nowhere.

3. Play the Game:
Grand Theft Desire

Slouched down in a vintage low-rider, you cruise the city. You've got a job to do, but that can wait. This is your world, you know it inside out, and everything and every place can be open to you. Stopping at a store, you buy new clothes; in a casino you lay down a bet; you go dancing at a club; and then you're back on the street, cruising. You look down at your muscular brown forearm, tattoos peeking out from under your shirt. You remember your date last night, starting with an innocent invitation to hot coffee and ending in bed with an impossibly proportioned woman who tells you, "You're the man." You *are* the man. You've got sex appeal and street respect and the points to prove it. Then you spot someone you recognize. You shoot him. As he falls you run over his body. Twice. An ambulance arrives, followed by a couple of police cruisers. You hop out of your car, machine gun in hand, shooting the medics and wasting the cops as your vehicle explodes behind you. Jumping in front of a passing sedan, you punch the driver in the head and pull her out, leaving her bleeding on the ground as you jack her ride. And then you reach for a can of Red Bull as you flex your thumbs, creaky and sore from hours of tapping console buttons while playing *Grand Theft Auto: San Andreas*.

As unlikely as it seems, progressives can learn a lot from a video game like this. But two things need to be recognized at the start of any discussion about its political possibilities. The first is that all the hand-wringing, wet-blanket, moralistic critics of video games are right: *Grand Theft Auto* is apocalyptically violent. In order to "win" the game a player has to shoot, beat, and run over literally thousands of individuals. Some of these people probably deserve it: gangbangers and killer cops, but firemen and medics and prostitutes are also fair targets, as is anyone who happens to be out on the street. Interaction with other characters in the game is, for the most part, limited to killing or setting up a killing and, to a lesser extent, having sex. It is Sigmund Freud's nightmare of unsublimated *eros* and *thanatos*, with a heavy emphasis on the latter: the return of the repressed expressed onscreen.

As Tim Winter, executive director of the Parents' Television Council, puts it, *Grand Theft Auto* is "lacking any redeeming social values."[1] The carnage in the game is justified by the thinnest of story lines: the main character returns to his home city after a long absence to find his mother murdered and his gang in disarray, and thus must avenge her death and get his gang back together. Yet most of the "missions" which make up the narrative play have little to do with this dubious revenge morality. The bulk of your playing time is spent making money and earning respect through crime, learning to make your way in the world with helpful hints like these:

— You can perform burglaries at night when not on a mission.

— Many homes can be broken into, and goods stolen from the
owners.[2]

The antisociality not programmed into the game is quickly provided by the adept player. An earlier version of GTA called *Vice City*
included a "cheat"—a programming quirk ostensibly not antici-
pated by the creators of the game—which allowed the player to
have sex with a prostitute and thus increase his life credits before
killing her to get his money back, thus retaining his virtual bank-
roll. A win-win situation.

If video games were just unredeemably violent it would be easy
for progressives to condemn or ignore them. But there is something else about these games, especially morally suspect ones
like *Grand Theft Auto*, that demands our attention. They are wildly
popular. According to the market research firm NPD, $9.9 billion
worth of video games were sold in the United States in 2004, out-
stripping the revenues from Hollywood box office sales.[3] *Grand
Theft Auto: San Andreas* led the pack that year, with over five million games sold; by July 2005 twelve million copies of GTA/SA had
been sold.[4] The game also out-rented all other video games its
first week of rental release, earning an unprecedented $1.6 mil-
lion in rental revenue in just seven days.[5] *Grand Theft Auto*, in all
its versions (*San Andreas* is the fifth), has sold more than 21 million copies since 2001, garnering $924 million in revenue for its
creator, Rockstar Games.[6]

Adding to these impressive numbers are countless pirated versions. A bootleg version of GTA/SA was available on the Web before it was even released, and among my gamer friends I'm alone
in having bought a copy.[7] It's true that most of those playing video
games are boys and men between the ages of fourteen and thirty-
four, but even within these parameters you have a lot of people

vicariously acting out a spectacular fantasy. More important, you have a lot of desires and dreams begging to be addressed. But in order to tap into that popularity, progressives first have to understand it.

So, what explains the appeal of a game like *Grand Theft Auto: San Andreas*? Perhaps Freud was right: we are libidinal animals after all and *GTA/SA* is a virtual arena in which to express eternal desires for sex and death we might otherwise play out dangerously on terra firma. It is not the healthy and constructive sublimation that Freud hoped for—sex into civilization and destruction into high culture—but it could be considered a sort of *desublimation*, a return to our basest desires which are then given release by role-playing in a virtual domain, similar to what Aristotle identified as the cathartic function of tragic drama.[8] Concerned parents' groups and crusading politicians likewise argue that video games tap into the dark landscape of our libidinal desires, but their fear is that these desires, once expressed in fantasy, will make the jump into the real world, resulting in violent and misogynistic behavior: two, three, many Columbines. This primal explanation, in either its cathartic or consequential form, may be part of the story, but only part.

Grand Theft Auto, like most popular video games sold today, is a role-playing game. Unlike the video arcade games of yesteryear, such as Pong or Pac Man, where the player manipulates paddles or pieces moving around a two-dimensional playing field, games like *GTA* drop the player into the position of a character roving about a three-dimensional world. Drawing their inspiration from the game *Dungeons and Dragons*, the earliest role-playing video games weren't much more than text and line drawings on a screen, asking players to type in their desired action—"turn left" or "grab sword"—and then responding with a new batch of text;

they counted on the imagination of the players to bring the world to life. As computer processor speed increased and graphics technology advanced, player imagination gave way to vivid virtual landscapes and the player entered the picture as a fully manipulatable avatar.

The first thing you notice when you play *Grand Theft Auto: San Andreas*, especially if you are white, middle class, and approaching middle age like myself, is that you are now young, poor, and black. You are CJ, a gangbanger living out a life of crime in the flats of a city that bears more than a passing resemblance to Los Angeles. You can change almost anything you want about your character: you can have him visit a barbershop and get a haircut, go shopping for new clothes, or get inked at a tattoo shop. If you feed CJ a lot of fast food his butt bloats up, making him a slow, soft target for rival gangbangers, or you can take him to the gym where he works out to get buff and tough. The one thing you can't change is his skin color.[9]

What does it mean that the best-selling video game in the world positions its player as a poor black man? It may mean very little: CJ isn't a real black man; he is an action-packing stereotype. He's the mythic gangbanger of a thousand and one rap songs which glorify thug life: "Life ain't nothin' but bitches and money," the group Niggaz With Attitude rapped in their hit song "Gangsta Gangsta," and this is CJ's creed.[10] The fact that the game starts off in a simulated Los Angeles in the early 1990s, the site of gangsta rap in its heyday, is no coincidence. The radio stations you tune in to as you drive in your car—which, this being simLA, you do most of the time—heavily favor late-eighties and early-nineties rap (along with amusing oddities like country singer Patsy Cline; a surreal soundtrack for a drive-by shooting). What the designers of *Grand Theft Auto* have delivered is the means to do what previous generations could only dream about: the ability to step into your favorite song. The popularity of playing CJ rides on the back of the immense popularity of gangsta rap music.

But it goes deeper than this. The attraction of the gangster stretches back to the glorification of Robin Hood and his bandit gang in Sherwood Forest, through the outlaws Butch Cassidy and the Sundance Kid, to today's TV mobster: Tony Soprano. It's the al- lure of the rebel, standing up to the powers-that-be—or, more ac- curately, the laws and mores those powers insist the rest of us live by. But the protagonist of *Grand Theft Auto* isn't just any old gang- ster, he's a *black* gangster. And in his rapacious appetite for sex and violence, CJ (and, by extension, the player) acts out the old stereo- type of black men as libidinally unrestrained. Part of the attraction of imagining yourself as a gangbanger in a gangsta rap song, or CJ in *Grand Theft Auto*, is identification with a Rousseauean noble sav- age, unbridled by the strictures of normal society, becoming the "white negro" hepcat immortalized by Norman Mailer in 1957.[11] That young, poor, urban black men enjoy playing GTA/SA as much as white, middle-class suburbanites shouldn't be too surprising. Stereotypes are believed (and desired) as fervently by those whom they are about as by those who use them to make sense of oth- ers. Black, white, brown, red, and yellow, it really doesn't matter; a part of all of us wants to be a nigga with attitude.

Amid this complicated morass of race and rebellion are open- ings for progressive politics. The first opportunity should be obvi- ous: the popular desire to rebel. The form of rebellion articulated in *Grand Theft Auto: San Andreas*—sticking it to the man through crime and violence—is far from progressive. It is predictable that rebellion has taken this form since it is legitimated and valorized by much of popular culture, from gangsta rap to cop shows on TV. But this isn't the only way that rebellion can be articulated.

What would it mean to reframe rebellion and freedom in political terms? Or rather, to frame progressive politics in the terms of dreams of rebellion?

This is not—necessarily—a call to revolution. Think of the most dignified and somber of protests, such as those staged by the Southern Christian Leadership Conference and led by Martin Luther King Jr. Black men and women, dressed in their Sunday best, peacefully picketing, marching on the side of a highway, confronting the bullhorns and dogs of Southern lawmen. These images represented the pacific dignity of otherwise law-abiding individuals, and that's how these protests have largely been remembered in our sanitized made-for-TV memory of the civil rights struggle. But the bigots on the White Citizens Councils who labeled these protesters radicals, agitators, and communists back in the late 1950s and early 1960s understood then what is glossed over now: those stately demonstrators *were* rebels. They were standing up to the (white) Man in front of a world media, and part of the power and attraction of those images was the inspiring example of rebellion.[12]

What image is cultivated by liberals and progressives today? Consider a press conference called by Senator Hillary Clinton in 2005: surrounded by heads of various liberal citizens' groups, she denounced *Grand Theft Auto: San Andreas* and asked for government investigation and regulation.[13] Forget for the moment that such gesticulations have about as much chance of success in slowing the popularity of video games as Nancy Reagan's "Just Say No" campaign had in preventing drug use in the 1980s. This solution is the old reformer's taboo denounced as ineffective by Walter Lippmann almost a century ago, and every public condemnation of *GTA* likely sends an extra thousand customers to the stores to buy the forbidden fruit. But the damage done by these well-meaning reformers is far more significant than this. Here is a group of well-mannered, well-dressed, liberal elites telling the rest of us, definitively, what is good and what is bad . . . and then calling on the government for regulation. It's almost a caricature of what the right believes about the left: we are busybodies who never saw a field of human experience that couldn't use help from the government—the condescending experts who tell people how to live their lives and then use our privilege and access to power to enforce our beliefs. The Establishment. Karl Rove himself could not have scripted a better press conference.

While liberals seem clueless, both the far left and right seem to understand better how to cultivate the image of rebellion. From the suave, pipe-smoking, masked Subcomandante Marcos issuing magical missives from the jungles of southern Mexico, to the revelry of the street protestors against the buttoned-down bureaucratic World Trade Organization, to the singing, praying "warriors for life" camped out in front of Terri Schiavo's hospital—like *Grand Theft Auto*, these forms of political expression articulate a popular dream of sticking it to the Man, with a certain style.[14]

Character identification in video games reveals deeper possibilities than merely identifying with the rebel. It signals a desire within us to identify with what we are not. In GTA this means acting out a racist stereotype like CJ, but it needn't be so limited. Identification with "the Other," whether that other be someone of a different race or station, or someone who embodies political options previously not considered, opens up new possibilities. The opportunity to walk, albeit virtually, in another's shoes expands the potential for understandings and alliances markedly different than those now manifested in typical progressive "coalitions" (many of which are nothing more than a list of organization names on a Web site or a piece of stationery). This identification with the Other is not the banal "respecting difference" of the multiculturalists: it entails *embracing* difference. It means transforming a distant object into an intimate subject.

Grand Theft Auto also teaches us that this identification with the Other can be experienced as a pleasure, not as a guilty chore. As I discuss in the next chapter, too much of progressive politics is done in the name, or for the benefit, of an abstract Other. This sort of progressive politics is experienced by the actor as a sacrifice of oneself for the betterment of someone else. (The recipient of these politics sees it the other way around: something done to them by someone else.) The Other is, by definition, foreign and incomprehensible, an object to be treated with charity or contempt, but always at a distance. Role-playing games suggest a popular desire to jump the gap and make the Other, literally, *identifiable* and thus not an "other" at all.

Again, this is emphatically *not* what *Grand Theft Auto* does. The Other the player becomes in the fantasy of *GTA* is itself a fantasy. CJ is a stereotype culled from centuries of racism and bandit worship, a gangsta rap antihero made virtual flesh. One might even argue that this allows the player to "other" his own rebellious tendencies, displacing them on to someone he is decidedly not. Still, the immense popularity of a game in which the player identifies with someone demonized as a menace to society says something about an untapped capacity for a politics which crosses boundaries of race, class, and ideology not through the liberal passivity of respecting and accepting—the "recognition of the other"—but through the more radical action of empathy with and activity as an Other.[15]

Video game theorists are split into two camps. "Narratologists" argue that what is important about video games is the story they tell. In the case of *Grand Theft Auto: San Andreas* this is the backstory of CJ's return to the hood and the tale that unfolds through the missions he must carry out in order to complete the game. In the end, a narratologist might argue, a good video game fosters identification with the protagonist and reads like a good novel (albeit one published in installments and sometimes read out of order). "Ludologists," on the other hand, argue that the game is the thing. What a character can do and how he or she can do it is what matters most, not the narrative path they follow. Academics like nothing more than to create rivalries, and to a certain extent this division is silly. Even Gonzalo Frasca, a game designer and academic who helped define the distinction with his site Ludology.org, believes that the division is "actually the product of confusion, stereotypes and disinformation."[16] Yet this division does call attention to the fact that two things drive video games: one, the character and the story he or she acts out; two, the quality of the action itself. In other words, how the game is played.

My own interest in video games began more than a decade ago when I was supposed to be writing my doctoral dissertation. Into the early morning I played a game called *Wolfenstein 3D* on my personal computer. Identifying with an Allied soldier trapped in a Nazi castle during World War II, I had to find and fight my way to freedom. Gunning down seemingly indestructible super-Nazis night after night, I shot a path through the castle and progressed from level to level, eventually winning my way to the end of the game and an unhappy return to my dissertation. I played *Wolfenstein* so much that it started to make its way into my dreams. But I never dreamed that I *was* the Allied soldier (a character even flatter than CJ), and I didn't feel the need to gun down threatening Nazis or complete any missions in my sleep. I did, however, have vivid dreams about walking through the vir-

tual maze of Wolfenstein castle; red brick hallways and slamming
steel doors became part of my nightly dreamscape. At the time, I
thought this was a singular experience; talking to other gamers
and reading about games since, I've realized that it wasn't. What
sticks with the player is not so much the story told, or even the
protagonist one identifies with, but the virtual world where the
player gets to play around in.

The world of *Grand Theft Auto: San Andreas* is immense. San
Andreas is a state, home to three cities. Los Alamos is Los Angeles.
Its streets are gritty, bright, and busy and lead to replicas of famous L.A. landmarks like the Santa Monica pier, the observa-
tory on top of Griffith Hill, or—in the most accurate of details—a
confusing snarl of freeways. To the north is San Fierro, a hilly simulation of San Francisco, complete with unpredictable weather
and heavy fog. To the west is Las Venturas, San Andreas's Las
Vegas, glowing with neon. Each city, in turn, is made up of neigh-
borhoods connected by miles and miles of streets. Around each
city lies countryside. Green rolling hills, forests, and farms accom-
pany you on the trip from Los Alamos to San Fierro, while the way
to Las Venturas is through miles of barren desert. Yet even in this
wilderness there are things to explore: small towns, truck stops,
fields of marijuana, and even a secret military base hiding UFOs.

In their popular industry textbook *Rules of Play: Game Design
Fundamentals*, Katie Salen and Eric Zimmerman call the virtual
world of video games the "magic circle."[17] Johan Huizinga, the renowned theorist of play who originated this term, used it to describe the space of games where outside rules are suspended and
rules of play are enforced.[18] Huizinga was thinking of the circle
drawn on the ground for a game of dice when he came up with
the expression, but as you walk, swim, bike, drive, fly, boat, and
hovercraft your way around San Andreas you can see why *Grand*

Theft Auto is so popular. The magic circle has been expanded into a magic world.

But it is not just the expanse of the virtual world of San Andreas that is so striking: it is its openness.[19] The freedom you have is astounding. One hundred eighty-seven "official" missions are required to complete the game, but there are countless sub-missions too. Some are necessary to move through the game faster and gain more autonomy. In order to fly a plane, for example, it's a good idea to go to flight school. But many options are not as instrumental. If you want, you can carjack a taxicab and pick up a fare, and then race to get the fare to his or her destination to receive a tip. You can put out fires with a stolen fire truck, or dis-tribute vigilante justice from a hot police car. Stepping into a club, you can learn to dance (and be subjected to praise or derision depending on how adept you are). And in a feature sure to please postmodernists, your video game character can play an eighties-era video game on his home TV.

You can also just while away your time customizing your character and his rides. Choice of haircut, clothes, and tattoos let you style CJ, and you can pimp your ride with new rims, up-holstery, and sound system. But customization just begins here. Recognizing the popular appeal of modification, video game de-signers regularly leave their program architecture *open*. In my day, gamers adept at programming built whole new levels of Castle Wolfenstein, posting their unofficial additions on the Internet for free downloading. This tradition has only expanded since that time. On a series of Web sites devoted to *Grand Theft Auto* you can download gamer-made "mods" for everything from an Adidas shirt for CJ to neon packs to under-light his rides. You can increase the texture of explosions or drop a game-era 1992 Honda Accord or 1986 Hummer into the play.[20]

By far the most popular mod is, or rather was, "Hot Coffee." Hot Coffee was a program patch which unlocked a minigame buried in *Grand Theft Auto: San Andreas*, ostensibly forgotten by the designers and discovered by a Dutch gamer in early summer 2005. With the software patch in place, CJ could follow a woman inside her house when invited for coffee. Once there, a minigame opened up which allowed CJ to have—and the player control—full-featured sexual intercourse, replete with porn movie dialogue. As might be expected, the discovery of Hot Coffee led to a new round of outrage, bringing Senator Hillary Clinton into the fray and leading Wal-Mart and Best Buy to temporarily pull the game from their shelves (proving that mass carnage is commercially acceptable but graphic sex crosses the line). After this bout of publicity, conveniently coinciding with the release of a new version of GTA/SA for the Xbox platform, Rockstar rereleased the game with the "error" fixed.[21]

Modifications and minigames aside, the real fun of playing *Grand Theft Auto: San Andreas* comes from just tooling around. When you play the game a little map pops up on the screen with a symbol directing you toward your objective. If you are trying to get to your buddy's house before he's wasted by a rival gang, you'll be led in the general direction until a hail of bullets lets you know you've arrived. But you don't need to do this. As you are headed to rescue your friend, you can simply take a left turn instead of the right you should have. Find an on-ramp to the freeway, and in a minute or so you'll be out in the country. You can stop your car, grab a dirt bike, and go for a ride through a forest, then ditch the bike and swim in a river. When you return, your homey will be pushing up daisies, but it doesn't really matter. If you want to, you can run the mission again. Or not.

All video games allow for a certain latitude of player agency—

that is, the player is always free to go left when it would have been better to go right. This agency is, of course, limited. As Janet Murray explains in her book on gaming, *Hamlet on the Holodeck*, players "can only act within the possibilities that have been established by the writing and programming."[22] In *Wolfenstein 3D* these possibilities were few and a wrong turn usually led quickly to a brick wall, but player autonomy has expanded dramatically in games like GTA/SA.[23] "It's about giving people freedom of choice," explains Dan Houser, Rockstar Games co-founder and an author of *Grand Theft Auto*. "It's still very much an action game, but there's also a whole world out there to explore."[24]

In a recent entry in his popular blog, game designer Greg Costikyan vented his frustration that innovative video game designers can't seem to get their games published while a routinely hyperviolent game starring the rap star 50 Cent is getting a heavy roll-out by the media giant Vivendi Universal: "They're morons and don't realize that the success of *GTA* is due to its noninstantial, open-ended, well-realized world and the gameplay it fosters."[25] Costikyan goes on to argue that it is this freedom of movement in the world, not the ability to play a violent thug like CJ, that explains GTA/SA's success. I don't think it is either/or. It is both the identification with the fantasized Other and the freedom to play with him that makes it such a hot game. But Costikyan is correct in arguing for the importance of open-ended gameplay. Without this freedom to explore, this openness, *Grand Theft Auto* would be just a badly rendered and interminably long music video.[26]

This concept of "gameplay" warrants political attention. If designers like Costikyan and the ludologists are right, then one of the key things that explains the popularity of a game like *Grand Theft Auto: San Andreas* is the experience a player has within the magic circle of the game. The scope of the world, the texture of the experience, and the autonomy of the action matter as much as if not more than whether the game is won or lost. (Winning is actually bittersweet, for once you win the game is over.) Means matter more than ends.[27]

What does this mean for progressives? Fashioning a politics that learns from and draws upon the popular attraction of video games means considering more than just end goals. Universal health care, free education, or a more equitable economy are worthy objectives. But we also have to give serious consideration to how we reach these targets—that is: *how we do politics*. We need to rethink progressive politics in terms of the quality of our gameplay. Perhaps one of the reasons progressive are not winning much these days is that lately our game isn't much fun to play.

In the interests of efficacy, a great deal of politics in recent years has been professionalized. Experts devise policies, lobbyists make the case to politicians, politicians fight for legislation, and lawyers file lawsuits in the courts to either enforce or overturn regulations. On the level of pure results it is a strategy that has worked well for progressives: much of the tangible progress in working conditions, protecting the environment, and attaining civil rights for women, minorities, and, to a lesser extent, gays has come from this professional model of political change. Think, for example, of the lawyer-driven landmark ruling of *Brown v. Board of Education* in 1954 that desegregated schools, or the environmental litigation and policies of the early 1970s that paved the way for the Environmental Protection Agency. But this strategy has a cost: it has made the game of politics a bore. It has separated the ends—life, liberty, and the pursuit of happiness for *all* citizens— from the means: an insider's game of reports, briefs, and bills. It has taken the game away from the very people for whom it is ostensibly being played.

In New York City (or Toronto, London, Dublin, or Vienna) it is hard to walk down a street these days without being asked by an earnest young woman or man with a clipboard if you are interested in saving the children, defending the environment, stopping the Bush agenda, or doing something equally worthy from a progressive standpoint. Witnessing such commitment is inspiring . . . until you stop and talk to the young "activist." You soon discover that they don't want your participation; they want your money to pay for someone else to participate for you. Explaining the good works that their organization will do, they ask you to agree to an automatic contribution each month. This is efficient. With regular donations, organizations like Greenpeace and Environmental Action, both of which engage in this sort of fundraising, can plan a budget and hire the policy analysts, lobbyists, and even street activists they need to effect social change.

But this method also severely circumscribes the playing field of politics, disconnecting potential activists from political *activity*. Young people recruited to save the environment find themselves working for third-party professional fund-raising companies.[28] Their participation is then limited to soliciting contributions for professional activists who do the real action. What is asked from the passerby is equally alienating: a contribution tagged to your credit card or bank account so that each month a few of your dollars disappear, silently, to do good in the world. This sort of politics discourages the creation of the very thing needed for democratic change: everyday citizen-activists. It also poisons the well for any citizen-activists legitimately registering voters, gathering signatures for petitions, or handing out information on the street: I now cross the street at the sight of a young person with a clipboard, as I'm sure others do when they see me with petition in hand. In Britain, where this sort of solicitation is widespread, they even have a word for these people: "chuggers," short for charity muggers. A survey in the United Kingdom showed that 84 percent of young people don't approve of the practice, with 70 percent saying that it just made them feel guilty.[29] This is not exactly a tactic aimed at winning over the masses for the cause. In pursuit of the most effective way to bring about worthy political ends, progressive organizations give too little thought to the politics of their means. They ignore the game. Again, the more ragtag groups further to the left on the political spectrum offer a glimpse of another way to do politics that might be applied on a larger scale.

On a Sunday mid-afternoon in early October 1998, more than a hundred young people have gathered at "the Cube," a large sculpture marking the entrance to Manhattan's East Village. Many of them carry radios tuned to a pirate radio station transmitting from an old bread truck parked nearby. Electronic dance music animates the crowd. Feet shuffle and heads bob. "Now," someone yells, and the group heads into the street, running west. One short block and we're on Broadway. A tall tripod is erected in the middle of the street and a person clambers to the top. A mobile sound system is wheeled out, tuned to the pirate station, and turned up to top volume. Broadway erupts into a party with brightly costumed dancers, fire-breathers and one particularly energetic fellow gyrating in a bright blue bunny suit. Leaflets are handed out proclaiming this as an action of the local chapter of Reclaim the Streets (RTS), thrown to protest New York mayor Rudy Giuliani's draconian "Quality of Life" campaign and the increased privatization of public space. But such assertions are redundant. The protest itself speaks more eloquently about reclaiming the streets for free and public expression than any photocopied piece of paper.[30]

For five years I was an organizer with the New York City franchise of the international direct-action group Reclaim the Streets.

RTS began in London in the early 1990s as an unlikely alliance between environmentalists and ravers, brought together in opposition to Britain's Criminal Justice and Public Order Act, which not only effectively outlawed political protests but also specifically targeted unpermitted parties with sound systems playing repetitive beats—in other words, raves. In response, Reclaim the Streets merged protests with parties, taking over streets and turning them into pulsing, dancing, temporary carnivals in their demand for public space.

The RTS protest model proved popular. From its relatively small first reclamation of Camden High Street in 1995, demonstrations grew steadily in size and scope. In July 1996, eight thousand people took over the M41 highway in an antiroad demonstration, and in April 1997, twenty thousand people descended upon Trafalgar Square in London to dance and protest the perceived vacuity of the general elections. Meanwhile, the Reclaim the Streets model spread to cities across the United Kingdom and Europe, then Australia, Israel, South America, and the United States.[31]

Acting autonomously, activists taking on the name of Reclaim the Streets adapted the London model to local conditions. In New York, RTS protested everything from the privatization of public space to the World Trade Organization, throwing demonstrations to draw attention to the destruction of community gardens and highlight the exploitation of Mexican American greengrocery workers. Political targets shifted with location and over time, but the method of protest—and the philosophy behind the method—remained constant. Reclaim the Streets believes that political ends must be embodied in the means you use. Giving the idea of "demonstration" new meaning, protests should literally *demonstrate* the ideal that you want to actualize. Therefore, a protest against privatization becomes a breathing, dancing example of what a liberated public space might look like. In our first action, RTS/NYC demanded collaboratively produced public space by going out and actually creating a collaboratively produced public space. When we protested the city government's destruction of community gardens, we did so by creating a garden (and garden party) in the middle of a busy street. How we played the game was as important—indeed, inseparable—from our goal.

This model and methodology were created in direct opposition to the experience that many RTS activists had had with traditional progressive protests. With the notable exception of ACT UP and its spin-offs, the dominant progressive protest model throughout the 1980s and 1990s was dull and deadly. It went something like this: Leaders organize a "mass" demonstration. We march. We chant. Speakers are paraded onto the dais to tell us (in screeching voices through bad sound systems) what we already know. Sometimes we sit down and let the police arrest us. We hope the mainstream media puts us on the news for five seconds. Sometimes they do; often they don't. While these demonstrations were often held in the name of "people's power," they were profoundly disempowering. Structured within this model of protest was a philosophy of passive political spectatorship: they organize, we come; they talk, we listen. And most of what was being said was negative and defeatist: "Hell No!" and "We're Against It!"

From the mid-1990s into the first years of the 2000s, Reclaim the Streets aspired to make protest politics a different experience. As RTS/NYC organizer William Etundi explains, "If you see people locking down and getting gassed, who wants to be part of that? But if you're shaking your body to a beat . . ." Etundi doesn't need to finish the sentence; his conclusion is obvious. Dancing is fun; waiting for the police to arrest you is not. "But it's more than this," he quickly adds. "Lockdowns and marches aren't the world we want to create. It's through our parties and our performances that we imagine liberation."[32] The goal of Reclaim the Streets was to create a lived imaginary—a magic circle.

The insistence that the purpose (and pleasure) of politics lies in the means as much as the ends did not begin nor end with Reclaim the Streets. At the beginning of the last century Mahatma Gandhi advised activists in India's anticolonial struggle against Britain to aspire to "be the change you want to see in this world." In the 1960s in the United States, creating a "beloved community" within and through organizing was a stated goal of the civil rights activists of the Student Nonviolent Coordinating Committee. But this model of politics might be used in everything from mass demonstrations to press conferences; it just entails thinking about the quality of the game.

This politics is also not without its dangers. Considering means as important as ends can slide into valuing means *in place of* ends. In her study of the antinuke movement of the 1980s, social movement scholar Barbara Epstein tells the story of one small protest group that blockaded an isolated, unused access road to a nuclear power plant even though the action had no impact on the facility's operation nor any chance of media coverage. What mattered to the activists was not efficacy but the principle of putting their bodies on the line—even if that line led nowhere.[33] Nor can every political goal be prefigured. How does one prefigure in protest the goal of unionizing workers? Working with the union UNITE! 169 and the Mexican American Workers Association, RTS/NYC gave it their best shot by staging raucous Mexican wrestling matches pitting a masked Superbarrio Man against *Rompe-Sindicatos Grandes y Pequeños* (Union Busters Great and Small) in the streets in front of union-busting greengrocers. But we were dramatizing justice—

Superbarrio Man inevitably triumphed—not embodying it. And not all political work is as fun as a street party. Stuffing envelopes, entering data on a computer, knocking on doors—a lot of politics is dreary, tedious, and time-consuming. "The trouble with socialism," Oscar Wilde once quipped, "is that it takes too many evenings." Wilde, a socialist himself, was half teasing, but only half. Still, progressive organizations make a serious mistake by not inviting the active participation of as many people as possible into even the more arduous parts of the game.

With 750,000 members, the Sierra Club is the largest environmental organization in the United States. It is also, like most progressive organizations, in trouble, with an aging and declining membership and less and less success on the ground. Recognizing this, the Sierra Club recently hired public policy expert Marshall Ganz to study their organization. His observations are illuminating. When the Sierra Club was founded back in 1892 it was part of a larger organizational culture of "voluntary associations," groups of individuals brought together for common purpose. So numerous and important were these groups to American life that nineteenth-century observers like Alexis de Tocqueville felt they were the bedrock of democracy. These associations depended upon their members not just for money but also for their activity. This sort of participation is still cultivated by certain organizations today. Most churches, for example, depend a great deal upon the activity of their congregations to sustain themselves. But this is less and less the practice among groups devoted to progressive causes. This is a real problem, warns Ganz. Advocacy groups, he argues, have become enchanted with efficiency, being "super-strategic" at the top rather than attending to their core values and engaging and activating their membership. The result is a declining and apathetic base, with environmentalism becoming less of a social movement and more a network of what Ganz calls "advocacy firms."[34]

Looking over the broad expanse of progressive organizations—as well as the Democratic Party—we might conclude that Walter Lippmann's dispirited dream of politics in the hands of an expert class has come to fruition. A cynic might respond that this is what most people want; that the vast majority of citizens don't want to *do* politics. At best we choose the goal we want and have someone else get us there; at worst we ignore the process altogether. Either way we're happy to have others play the game for us.

But I don't believe it has to be this way. The intense pleasure gamers get out of playing games like *Grand Theft Auto* suggest that if a game offers power, excitement, and the room to explore, people will play evening after evening after evening, almost regardless of the results. Perhaps the problem is not that people don't want to get involved in politics, but rather that they don't want to take part in a professionalized politics so interested in efficiency that there is no space for them, or they don't want to spend time in a political world so cramped that there's no freedom to explore and discover, to know or master. People don't get involved in politics because the process, both figuratively and literally, does not involve them.

Video games demand the participation of the gamer. This is true for most media. Books, for example, demand the attention and imagination of the reader. But there is also a critical difference. As *Grand Theft Auto*'s Dan Houser explains, "books tell you something. Movies show you something. But games let you *do* something."[35] And in video games this participation is taken to a different level as the game itself changes with the participation of the spectator. In *GTA* new worlds open up to the player as he or she develops new skills, and characters respond based upon the player's past actions. This happens according to fixed algorithmic computer program rules and within the confines of the "magic circle," yet even with these limitations the player is a real participant in the game, enabling something game designers Salen and Zimmerman call "transformative play."[36] In video games, unlike almost all other mass media, the spectator also becomes a producer.

Turning spectators into producers was something we tried to do in Reclaim the Streets. Like the mass globalization protests of recent years, what we were really organizing was a framework for activity. We decided upon a place and time and put out a call. We printed propaganda and press releases, trundled in a sound system, and set up legal teams to get people out of jail if they got arrested. But the actual shape the protest took on was determined by who showed up and what they did. Who could have planned on a man dressed in a bright blue bunny suit?

Building a protest with an open architecture, we encouraged player modification. We saw what we were doing as opening up a space—literally, in terms of reclaiming a street from auto traffic and specialized use, but also metaphorically, by opening up a space for people to explore what political activism could mean for themselves. As long as they were nonviolent—our one rule, ruthlessly policed—participants could take a left instead of a right, follow our mission, or just tool around. In this, Reclaim the Streets encouraged what the Situationists, an earlier generation of French activist intellectuals, championed as the *dérive*—literally, drifting, and, in their words, "a practice of a passional journey out of the ordinary through rapid changing of ambiances."[37] It is a good, if a bit obtuse, description of what occurs at RTS events (and, for that matter, what happens while playing video games).

Reclaim the Streets' commitment to individuals' exploration

sometimes led to chaotic, seemingly unfocused demonstrations, a criticism also leveled against later globalization protests. But it also resulted in demonstrations, in both senses of the word, of exuberant political participation.[38] "Games [are] inherently inefficient," video game designers Salen and Zimmerman explain in their popular textbook.[39] So is the open-ended, participatory, modifiable politics of Reclaim the Streets and many direct action groups today. This makes for a messy sort of politics, but also a game with room to play.

It may seem naive to suggest that a model employed by fringe protest groups and embedded within video games could be adopted by massive organizations like the Sierra Club, not to mention a behemoth like the Democratic Party. But recent progressive initiatives like MoveOn.org show the promise of moving these practices into mass politics. Founded in 1998 by Joan Blades and Wes Boyd, two Silicon Valley entrepreneurs frustrated by the inability of Congress to "move on" past the Clinton sex scandal, MoveOn is a now a multi-issue progressive organization with over 3.3 million members. Two things mark it as unique. One, MoveOn engages its membership via regular e-mail messages in everything from letter writing campaigns to soliciting advice on whether to endorse a presidential candidate. They poll their members regularly, and the organization takes stands, or doesn't, based on the response. In a word, they give their members a sense of agency. Two, outside of a Web site, an e-mail membership list, and a small staff, MoveOn doesn't really exist. It is a virtual organization whose primary resource is the activity, and creativity, of its members.

A good example of this is the group's "Bush in 30 Seconds" contest. In November 2003 MoveOn announced that it was looking to create a thirty-second television advertisement criticizing the president's politics and policies. Instead of going the usual route of hiring media professionals, MoveOn turned to its amateur membership, asking them to use their handicams and desktop editing software (or access to moonlit professional facilities) and create an ad themselves. More than fifteen hundred advertisements were submitted. MoveOn posted more than a thousand of these ads on their Web site and invited their membership to rate them. Over a two-week period, 110,000 people visited the site and viewed the ads, posting more than 2.9 million comments in response. A simple, powerful advertisement composed of silent scenes of somber children at work in menial jobs, with the tagline "Guess who's going to pay off President Bush's $1 trillion deficit?" submitted by a former Republican named Charlie Fisher, was chosen by both popular acclaim and the judgment of the staff of MoveOn. It was broadcast on TV the week of the president's State of the Union address. The money to air the advertisement was easily solicited from the very same audience that submitted and judged the entries. People give generously to what they feel they are a part of.[40]

Asking its members to design and submit video clips criticizing the Bush administration is perhaps not as efficient as hiring an ad firm with its design team, production facilities, and focus groups, but as a process it engages (and entertains) a large body of people. It also resulted in a low-cost, high-quality product and the donations required to get it broadcast. MoveOn works because it invites its members to play.

MoveOn is a promising start, but there's still a long way to go. To embrace a politics that recognizes the allure of the Other and the power of rebellion, that understands that it is not just winning or losing that matters but how the game is played, that privileges exploration and modification—all this requires a significant shift from the efficient, professionalized "downsizing of democracy" that political scientists Matthew Crenson and Benjamin Ginsberg argue has become the status quo state of politics over the past century.[41] Change, however, has to happen. Ironically, when we privilege efficient ends over participatory means, the ends eventually become unattainable. The great strength of democracy is that it depends upon its players. They can be treated as outside spectators for only so long. Sooner or later they will want to play, and if progressives have not devised a game that engages and excites them, they'll go play elsewhere.

There's one more little lesson progressives can learn from *Grand Theft Auto*: not all fun has to be politically correct. I think of myself as a reasonably nonviolent guy, not any more or less misogynistic than the average man brought up in this society. Yet playing games like *GTA*, I find I enjoy engaging in virtual acts that I've spent most of my life condemning in the real world. Does this make me a hypocrite? Or merely complicatedly human? The refusal to accept that people are complex beings, with contradictory ideals of reality and fantasy (a refusal that often results in the ignorance, avoidance, or repression of the latter), is a hangover from the old Enlightenment ideal of authenticity, the dream of a seamless self.

Whether a manifestation of primal instinct or the result of growing up in a violent, sexist, and racist society, we have desires that are, well, less than desirable. It does no good to condemn these feelings, insisting that people must not think bad thoughts. This way leads to hypocrisy and self-deception and a politics obsessed with purity and authenticity. More to the point, it results in a politics with very few adherents.[42] We have to make peace with our desires—violent, racist, and sexist as they may be—and find safe expression for them. *Grand Theft Auto: San Andreas* is one such expression. It is not the job of progressives to condemn popular fantasy and desire. It is our job to pay careful attention to them, learn from them, and perhaps—God forbid!—even enjoy them ourselves. Then carjack these desires and fantasies and drive them someplace else.

4. Think Different:
Advertising Utopia

Dressed in a suit and tie, a man steps out of his car. The front door of his house bursts open and a young girl runs out, throwing herself into the arms of her father. Father and daughter, bright and happy, get back into the car and drive to a fast-food restaurant. In the drive-through lane they are cheerily handed neat white bags of food. The next scene shows them strolling through an open gate and into a zoo, the man without his tie and jacket, the child giddy with excitement. The day is beautiful, the sun shining; daughter feeds father a french fry as they sit together on a park bench. The girl points out an elephant and its calf walking by. Father and daughter share a moment, witness to the universality of generations, watching the old leading the young and passing on the wisdom (and, presumably, consumption habits) of the ages. The last shot shows father and daughter walking hand in hand, a pink balloon tethered to the girl's wrist and floating above them, a drink cup in the man's free hand, drawing this idyllic late afternoon to a close. In the lower right-hand corner of the screen, the McDonald's golden arches logo appears.

It is a specific advertisement for a specific company, but we've seen it a thousand times before, a thousand times since, and selling a thousand different products. It makes the same promise that all advertisements make: a fantasy world is only a product purchase away. Progressives have traditionally looked at advertising with disgust, for good reason: ads clutter up our roadsides and interrupt our TV shows; they create unreal expectations and convince us to buy what we don't really need. They are a symbol of the waste—and bad taste—of consumer capitalism. But there's also another reason we progressives are suspicious of advertising: ads make their pitch not to our heads but to our hearts (or anatomy a bit lower). They argue their case without rational argument, appealing to us in a deeply visceral and personal way. Advertising speaks to desire, not reason.

The traditional progressive response to the fantasies of Madison Avenue is reactionary. We're against it, and we want to oppose it with what we know: reason. We must cultivate "defenses against the seduction of eloquence," argued the late, great critic of commercialism Neal Postman.[1] For Postman and many other critics, the principal weapon in this defense is *media literacy*. The vulnerable masses will be schooled in the rhetoric of marketing in order to "read" and interpret advertising as we once learned to read and interpret the word. However, more than a quarter century of media literacy curricula in grade school and scores of PBS specials debunking advertising has resulted in little other than a generation of knowing educators, savvy spectators, and advertisers who have adapted to our new media smarts with commercials that incorporate an ironic wink.

Perhaps there are other ways for progressives to think about advertising. We need to burrow deep into it, drilling past the sizzle into the steak. There we'll find its DNA, the code that guides its various permutations, no matter what product is being sold. From these building blocks I believe we can reassemble a model of communication and persuasion that is true to progressive ideals *and* effective in today's world. In brief, we need to heed the call of Apple Computer's grammatically challenged campaign and "think different" about advertising.

All advertising is about transformation. The product advertised will transform you from what you are (incomplete, inadequate, and thoroughly normal) into what you would like to be (fulfilled, successful, and completely special). This philosophy underlies the classic before-and-after advertisement. There are two pictures: on the left is a loveless loser with stained teeth and bad breath, on the right is the same person, now radiant and alluring with a Pepsodent smile, magically transformed. This is a primitive variant, and one we tell ourselves we'd never fall for today, but the same logic underlies nearly all advertising, even if "before" is only assumed. In this way, art critic John Berger reminds us, advertising is never about the present, always the future.[2]

Consider the McDonald's ad. The promise here is that McDonald's will transform your family (busy, alienated, normal) into the McDonald's family (carefree, harmonious, superior). Which would you rather be? This logic applies itself not only to the characters but to the setting as well. The mise-en-scène of advertisements—the tropical islands and hip clubs, efficient fast-food drive-throughs and zoos where no money changes hands—have meaning only as a transformation of places we are all too familiar with: cold streets, nights in front of the TV, wretched restaurants, and privatized public spaces. This is the utopian promise of advertising: somewhere out there is a world far superior to the one we inhabit, where the person we'd like to become resides. And it is all obtainable. The means to the ends are ridiculous—a world transformed through a hamburger—and this is what makes advertising absurd. It is also what makes it so successful, for with each promise not delivered, the frustrated consumer looks elsewhere for gratification. If not a burger, then maybe a toothpaste will make me who I want to be. Failing that, there's always that bottle of Courvoisier XO.

In an increasing number of ads today the transformation imagined or the dream portrayed (if there is any at all) is often patently ridiculous. The 2006 ads for Axe men's deodorant that overtly promise an "axe effect" of immediate female supplication come to mind. These spots, and others like them, acknowledge that the utopian promises of advertising are widely understood to be absurd. But within this new strategy is another recognition: that there's really no other competition out there; no other dreams being promised, so one might as well sit back, laugh, and be entertained.

Transformation was once the property of progressives. It was the great conservative Edmund Burke, after all, who railed against the French Revolution because the pace of republican progress promised to upset the time-tested tradition of divine right and natural hierarchy. What were democracy, socialism, anarchism, civil rights, and feminism if not dreams of a world transformed? Advertising is, in essence, a promise. A promise of transformation. It is often a false promise, sometimes an ironic promise, but a promise nonetheless. Progressives need to work on our promises.

If we reemploy this promise of transformation, what distinguishes us from Madison Avenue? The difference is that the transformation we promise is not magical, or at least not entirely so. I have yet to come across an explanation for how a hamburger can give me free afternoons, bring me closer to my children, or make the sun shine on a clean and free public space. The reason is simple: it can't. There is no connection between the product and those desires. However, it is quite simple to connect all sorts of progressive policies and politics to the McDonaldland utopia. Shorter workweeks and flextime can offer free afternoons—and lower unemployment.[3] Legislation that provides for generous paternity leave for men and maternity leave for women sets the stage for early child-parent bonding and legitimates co-parenting. And generous funding of parks, museums, and zoos will ensure that our public spaces are clean, safe, and free. All these issues are currently being fought for by a variety of progressive organizations and politicians, yet the reasoning offered is usually cold, logical, and analytic: percentages, populations, and numbers of hours lost and gained. The vision propagated is often a gloom-and-doom dystopic scenario of what happens if the other side wins and takes away what little we have left. What is there to dream about in this?

We progressives too often pitch our cause in reactionary terms of hanging on to what we have and holding the line. Or we make appeals to guilt and sacrifice, asking people to give up what they already have so that others might have a piece of it. These are appeals to the past or to a diminished present. They take for granted that the best we can do is redistribute what we have already attained and that we cannot all gain more. Because of this they are doomed to failure. For a moment imagine an advertisement that asks you to stay where you are, to accept things as they are, or, if you are looking for social change, promises to make things personally worse for you. This is what progressives often do and, tactically speaking, it is insanity.[4]

Instead of asking for sacrifice, we could try appealing to people's hopes and dreams, weaving them into a tale that ends with their lives being better than they are now. Why not envision the transformed world that progressive politics might deliver? We already have a model: with all references to fast food purged, the commercial aired by McDonald's makes an excellent advertisement for a progressive social agenda.

Advertising works because its message is personalized, always directed toward the individual watching: "This Bud's for You," "Have It Your Way at Burger King," "My Life. My Card," "Which iPod Are You?" As Stuart Elliot, the *New York Times* correspondent on all things advertising, notes: "Madison Avenue has become obsessed with using the word 'my'—along with 'your' and 'our.'" Personalization is the key that unlocks the door between the product and the consumer; it is how to get consumers not just to buy an item but, in the words of a VP for branding at Coca-Cola (viz. MyCoke.com), "make it their own."[5]

In the prehistory of modern advertising, products were sold primarily through mass appeals to an anonymous public. A late-nineteenth-century ad for Ivory Soap, for instance, illustrated a bar of soap with the modest tagline: "An agreeable item of toilet use." Over the next few decades the pitch began to change. In the 1930s Lifebuoy was selling soap with a picture of a man at his desk, two women sharing a conspiratorial secret behind him, and the directed question: "Are People Whispering Behind Your Back?" Implied, of course, is that you are the odorous person that others whisper about. Applied more subtly today, this technique of directed personal identification is still a mainstay of advertising. Recall again the McDonald's commercial. The father and daughter may be a bit happier than we are, their zoo a bit cleaner than the one in our town, and their life is no doubt a bit better than our own, but we can also recognize ourselves in them. They laugh; we've laughed before. They get along; every once in a while we do, too. And, of course, thanks to the near ubiquity of McDonald's, we can eat a meal identical to theirs. Unless we can identify our (real and imagined) life with the one being played out before us, the advertisement doesn't work. And so we are made to feel what we know cannot be true: that an advertisement broadcast to millions and a product manufactured for a mass market speaks just to us. As the latest McDonald's slogan goes: "I'm lovin' it."[6]

Progressives have a tendency to make their appeals in the name of abstract others: The People, The Masses, The Tired and Poor. Boycott grapes and you'll help The Farm Workers, or stop the war in Iraq to prevent the slaughter of Innocent Iraqis or American Soldiers. There is nothing wrong with sympathizing with the plight of other people; an injury to one is an injury to all. But if advertising can teach us anything it is that the people being addressed have to be able to see themselves in the narrative being told; they need to imagine how *their* lives will be impacted if they use our soap, or climb on board with our politics. Yet progressive policy is often cast in its potential impact on a social body like the working class, women, or Latinos, or even on a social problem like the environment or civil rights. A mass solution for a problematic mass. By pitching our politics and programs in terms of the needs of abstractions, we end up recognizing the desires of no one in particular.

Not even our own. Deep down in the progressive psyche is the haunting suspicion that our needs and desires can be neither universalized nor politicized. *We* are individual, unique, and special; *they* are The People (a category both noble and empty). Our passions must be kept private while we articulate those of a generic other. This refusal to root a politics in our own particular passions alienates progressives. If we are afraid to publicly recognize and politicize our own desires, how can we hope to speak to those of other people? But if we start to ask the questions of what our needs and desires are, and how a politics might meet them, we just might discover that, lo and behold, *our* needs are the same as *theirs*.

It is natural for advertisers to address the individual. They want individual people to buy individual products, and their model world is composed of individual units in pursuit of self-gratification. As conservative Prime Minister Margaret Thatcher once asserted: "There is no such thing as society. There are individual men and women."[7] Progressives don't share this vision of the world. We tend to see the world in more collective terms: social forces shape history and political progress comes through collaborative social action. Solidarity is our means and community is the end. It wasn't sheer idiocy that led progressives to adopt the habit of speaking in abstractions and appealing to groups; it flows from our understanding of the world. But it is a worldview that needs some work. There's nothing wrong with the goals of community and solidarity, but we need to acknowledge that this may not be how people currently *experience* their world. There is more than a grain of truth in Thatcher's words. People experience social forces and social change on a personal level. Think of taking part in a large protest or political rally. The exhilaration evoked is felt by everyone else in the crowd, and the goal of the event can only be brought about by acting with others, but no mass can feel for you or be constituted without you (*that* is the fantasy of Fascism). The point of reception—even in a crowd, even working with others—is the individual.

Progressives need to frame their appeals so that they resonate with individuals. The practice should not be limited to using personally directed appeals to market this policy or that candidate to this or that individual. That is the business of advertisers, and one we shouldn't neglect, but we need to push the principle of person-

alization further and engage the individual in the political process itself. In the mid-1990s I helped start a community activist
group in Lower Manhattan called the Lower East Side Collective
(LESC). All of our "advertising" followed a simple format designed
by Leslie Kauffman, now a staff organizer with United for Peace
and Justice. On the front of a flyer we would briefly explain the issue we were building a campaign around, whether it was fighting
rent-law decontrol or saving community gardens. On the back,
under the headline "What Can I Do?" we would list five things that
the reader could do to get involved, from "If you have five minutes
a week" (usually a couple of phone calls to key politicians) to five
minutes a day (letters and faxes) to five hours a week (join us).
By creating this menu of scalable involvement, LESC personalized
the activity of politics by offering the opportunity and direction
for people to become individual political agents, while recognizing
that people have important personal lives outside of politics.

Many progressive organizations claim to be participatory but
then demand that participants play out the role of an idealized,
frequently selfless, activist. LESC tried something different by allowing people to personalize how they participated in our campaigns. Participation didn't just mean more people to make more
phone calls; it meant opening up our organization to new voices
and new ideas and tailoring our tactics to make use of individual
personalities and proclivities. (And since people did feel personally involved in the organization, we ended up with a lot of people
making phone calls too.) This openness took LESC in directions
that the founders hadn't planned. I, for one, couldn't have cared
less about community gardens, yet that became one of our liveli-
est and most successful campaigns. More important, connecting
to people at the point of their own passions, and with an under-

standing of their own limitations, infused the group with an energy and creativity (and absence of guilt-tripping) that's rare to find in a progressive community organization. People didn't feel like they had to be someone else to participate in politics; they were valued for being themselves—and then given opportunities to transform themselves into the active citizens they hoped to become.

The Lower East Side Collective is hardly the first left-liberal group to bank on the individuality of its members, nor is it the last (this is a hallmark of contemporary e-organizations like MoveOn.org), yet the personalization of the political process is something that needs continual cultivation. Because progressives believe so fervently in society, individualization will always be a more complicated and difficult task for us than for advertisers, or conservatives. But unless we learn to personalize our politics, our victories will be as fictional as the abstractions we've created to fight them.

Advertising also requires us to "think different" about the very way we think. We like to think we derive our truths through linear logic: A plus B results in C. As if solving a math equation, you move from left to right, adding up the statements, and at the end you get a nice, neat, provable sum. But apply this logic to the earlier advertisement: A father and daughter, plus McDonald's, equals familial nirvana. According to the laws of linear logic this is an absurd conclusion. None of us would stand for such manipulative reasoning. But the trick of advertising is its ability to circumvent this linear logic, substituting associations for equations.[8] A picture of a happy family is placed next to a picture of McDonald's. Bingo: Big Macs *are* familial bliss. The goal is to equate unlike items, collapsing difference into unity. The great Soviet filmmaker Sergei

Eisenstein may have been the first to understand the power of the quick edit and juxtaposition, but it is advertisers who have mastered this technique.[9]

In recent years, association has become a mainstay of advertising technique, eclipsing the dubious linear logic that propped up the old "before and after" model of advertising past (while still retaining the goal of magical transformation). Looking over the advertisements represented by the recent winners of the industry's Clio awards, it is hard to find an example that is anything but associations of dissimilar subjects. Budweiser, the Gold Medal winner in 2004 for the Television/Cinema category, advertises its low-calorie beer with a "real men of genius" series, poking gentle fun at the social foibles and everyday stupidity of the regular guy: wearing too much bad cologne, eating taco salads, passing gas, and so on. The product appears only in the last, disconnected scene, in which a bottle of Bud Light is pulled from an ice chest.[10] What is the association? Drink Bud and you'll smell bad? This is an evolution (or devolution) of the more primitive association displayed in the McDonald's commercial. The link is no longer between the product advertised and what the consumer would like to become, but between the viewer and the advertisement itself. In ad after ad, scenes are played out that are funny, clever, sexy, ironic, shocking, or disgusting. The objects of association don't matter; merely a response on our part, any human response—a smile, gasp, thought, cry of recognition, or just appreciation for being entertained—is what the advertiser wishes us to associate with the product.[11]

How can progressives hope to appropriate such a principle as association? Why would we want to? To answer the second question first, we must. Linear logic belongs to the age of the sentence and the paragraph; associative logic is in tune with the present visual era. If progressives wish to communicate in the present, they need to learn the language of association. Conservatives use it all the time. Think of the propaganda of the second Bush administration in preparation for their war in Iraq. By constantly referring to Iraq in the same sentence as terrorism, and Saddam Hussein in the same breath as al-Qaeda, the administration effectively forged an association that continues today. In fact, when the Bush administration tried to prove "logically" the connection between Hussein and weapons of mass destruction (WMD)—Secretary of State Colin Powell's infamous presentation at the United Nations regarding the nuclear capability of Hussein—it backfired when the evidence turned out to be faked and no WMDs were found. Association, on the other hand, can never be found false because it makes no truth claims.

But is this what we want to do? Elide the truth and play a cynical game of realpolitik? I don't think progressives have to. There is a way in which to harness the power of association without slipping into a moral morass. Associations conjure up an ideal, not an equation of facts. But this does not mean that associations must be built upon lies.

Association can be specious—McDonald's and family, or al-Qaeda and prewar Iraq—but associations do exist between seemingly unconnected objects or subjects. Exciting work in physics in the fields of chaos and complexity theory, and in biology around biodiversity, argues for the fundamental interdependency of seemingly discrete categories. You don't have to believe, as meteorologist Edward Lorenz first put it, that the flutter of butterfly's wings in Beijing could create a tornado in Texas to acknowledge that we are wired into a complex ecological and social system, with lines of connection and association that are not immediately apparent.

Lines of connection and association have been traced by progressives before. These were the lines that Martin Luther King Jr.
wanted us to follow when he asked us to consider where we get
our sponges, our soap, our coffee, tea, and toast: "Before you finish
eating breakfast in the morning you are dependent on more than
half of the world."[12] Associations were what King was describing
late in his life when he drew out the connections between the war
in Vietnam and poverty and race hatred in the United States.[13]
More recently, Ted Nordhaus and Apollo project pioneer Michael
Schellenberger, in their provocative 2004 white paper "The Death
of Environmentalism," argue that the environmental movement needs to articulate a wider set of associations, articulating
(and publicizing) links between industry and weather, resources
and war, nature and values. Peter Teague, in his preface to this
report, explicitly scolds the environmental movement for not
making public sooner the invisible but real associations between
global warming and contemporary natural catastrophes like
deadly hurricanes.[14]

But, as the authors of the white paper go on to argue, progressives also need positive associations. It's not enough to draw connections between things we do not like; associations can also
communicate what we are for and what kind of world our policies
might create. And we can do this ethically and honestly. Back to
our McDonald's advertisement: what if progressives ran the same
spot? A father picks up his daughter in the afternoon and they
have a wonderful day at the zoo. Same idyllic scene, same light-
ing, same music, same smiles, same personalization. Then, at the
end, instead of golden arches popping into view there would be
a tagline calling for a reduced workweek, a tax increase on the
wealthy to pay for clean and safe public parks, or even a plea to
bring our troops back from Iraq to be with their families. Which

associations have more validity: ours or McDonald's? The same utopian dream is being sold—not through painstaking explanation but using juxtaposition, editing, and association. But our associations have an integrity to them which those of commercial advertising do not. The principle of association is an opportunity for progressives to move past the timid linear logic that inspires no one and to harness a powerful tool of persuasion.

Association can be employed at the level of organization building as well. In the Lower East Side Collective we didn't fund-raise by applying for grants, sending out direct-mail appeals, or badgering people on the street. Instead, we raised money for our organization by throwing huge, raucous dance parties. We goofed around and socialized while tabling for causes, we prided ourselves on our cleverly worded signs, and, working with groups like Reclaim the Streets and More Gardens!, we turned our demonstrations into festive carnivals. In brief, we enjoyed ourselves. This wasn't hard to do, but it also wasn't an accident. As the last line of LESC's introductory flyer read: "We believe politics can be fun."[15]

The projection of "fun" was part of a conscious strategy on our part to counteract the public perception of leftists as dour, sour, and politically correct—a stereotype that had some validity, at least in the Lower East Side of Manhattan in the mid-1990s. "Changing the culture of the Left" was how Alice Meaker Varon, the main architect of this strategy, put it.[16] Leslie Kauffman went so far as to prepare an organizational instruction sheet for LESC activists with characters like "Sullen Sue" and "Ideological Ivan" as anti-inspirational warnings. And LESC had a standing working group whose function was fun. We called it, with tongue firmly in cheek, the "Ministry of Love." Within a year of our founding we had more than fifty activists working with us and were engaged in six simultaneous campaigns. We received an award for innovative organizing from the Abbie Hoffman Foundation. We also had been attacked by several on the sour left for being too joyous. That's when we knew we had succeeded in transfoming the association of progressive activism from sacrifice to pleasure; we changed the game, at least for a short time and in a small place.

The importance of fun in politics is not just the luxury of the privileged activist. In the middle of the murderous civil war in El Salvador, Salvadoran women would immediately create three committees when setting up new refugee camps: one on sanitation and construction, another on education, and a third, *comité de alegría*, on joy.[17] This is not to say that there are not also real associations between activism and sacrifice. The politico sacrifices free time as well as the bliss of ignorance. But activism is also social, exhilarating, rebellious, and fun. Which make better selling points? Associations are built as much as they are revealed, and if progressives hope to appeal to anyone outside of a small group of self-flagellants and the terminally self-righteous, we need to cultivate and articulate positive associations with progressive politics.

Building associations between progressives and good times may seem trivial (the dour doctrinaire in myself even winces writing these words), but it is not: these associations communicate the personality of the politics we are trying to actualize. In marketing parlance, they make up the progressive *brand*. Branding is the hot new buzzword in advertising, but its practice stretches back at least a century to Standard Oil and its consolidation of many small refineries within one highly recognizable entity. Today it is commonplace for products and services, often unlike in form and function and manufactured by myriad subcontractors scattered across the globe, to be bestowed with a robust and easily identifiable personality with its own set of associations: the energetic Exxon (Standard Oil) tiger, Coke as the "real thing," and so on.

Kevin Roberts, CEO of the advertising giant Saatchi & Saatchi, recently "branded" his own brand of branding. He calls these "lovemarks," differentiating them from traditional brands by the "emotional resonance" they conjure up in consumers with their sense of "mystery, sensuality and intimacy." The goal of these lovemarks is to foster, in the Saatchi CEO's words, "Loyalty Beyond Reason."[18] (No doubt this phrase would sound better in German.) The concept behind Roberts's "lovemarks" is nothing new for corporate America. In the early years of the last century, American Telephone and Telegraph had to figure out how to convince the public that a private monopoly of a public utility would be in the citizenry's best interest. William Banning, AT&T's assistant publicity manager, put it this way in a 1923 company memo: "[Our job] is to make the people understand and love the company. Not merely be consciously dependent upon it—not merely regard it as a necessity—not merely take it for granted, but to love it—hold real affection for it."[19] Astute executives have long understood that the emotional relationships that form between brands and people are critical to the success of corporations.

Politics are also branded. Think of the associations one makes when hearing the term "conservative." There are all types of conservatives: fiscal conservatives who believe in budgetary restraint, religious conservatives who believe that law should flow from the word of God, cultural conservatives who want to hold on to the old ways, and even neoconservatives who believe in revolutionizing nearly everything (except the profit principle). Yet they all come together in a brand. For progressives this brand has negative connotations and for conservatives it resonates positively, and each side fights to make its definition the prevailing one in the public mind. In recent years conservatives have won this battle. One of the great feats of American politics in the last half century is the transformation of the conservative brand from one associated with greedy industrialists and the economic failures of Herbert Hoover to one of the middle-class David standing up to the Goliath welfare state.

Whereas conservatives have embraced—and succeeded at—branding, progressives are still shy. In part this is because in branding we recognize commodity fetishism at its most extreme with the simplification and substitution of the imaginary for the complex real. But progressives also chafe under the yoke of a brand because of our own fetishization of difference. We, progressives argue, are a variegated rainbow that cannot be reduced to a monochromatic brand. The problem is that progressives have already been branded. Unwilling to sully our hands with the task ourselves, we have been branded by our adversaries. Liberals are emotional, weak, and elitist; leftists are loony and dangerous; both are out of touch with the mainstream. This brand is then spread and reinforced by a mass media. In the absence of a self-representational brand, and needing a shorthand way to communicate complexity, the media really has no other option.

To brand ourselves, we need to learn from corporations, asking ourselves how they devise a personality that encompasses the diversity of their products. This doesn't have to mean a snow job. Yes, British Petroleum has rebranded itself as an eco-friendly flower and purged that icky "petroleum" from its initials (as well as the nationalistic "British"), and Citibank would like us to believe that they represent the leading edge of antimaterialism, but a good brand can also accurately represent what is being produced and how it is being done. In other words, a progressive brand could honestly encapsulate and communicate what we stand for and how we want to change the world. In recent years, even corporate America has made forays into branding that represents the actual workings of the company. A few years back, Saturn Motors ran a series of ads introducing their consumers to the workers who made and sold their autos, and American Apparel branded itself as the antisweatshop clothing manufacturer with profiles of its workers and explanations of its labor philosophy.[20] These, of course, are as much an idealization of the production of its products as they are real explications, but the success of both campaigns demonstrates that the brand need not detach itself entirely from reality; it can be a sign of itself rather than a sign which disguises itself. A transparent brand.

What might a progressive brand look like? Roosevelt's New Deal immediately comes to mind. Under these two evocative words stood a whole battery of economic, political, and cultural initiatives. The Civil Rights Movement is another good example, organizing an array of grievances, solutions, strategies, and organizations under one label. And the Rainbow Coalition, assembled for Jesse Jackson's 1984 presidential run, was an attempt to brand the very diversity of the progressive movement (albeit a marginally successful one). In his popular book *Don't Think of an Elephant*, George Lakoff argues that progressives need to better frame their politics to give them coherence. He suggests that progressives' politics can be made sense of through the metaphor of the "nurturant parent" (conservatives, he argues, are best represented by the "strict father"). Nurturant Parent is a brand. One can question whether it is the best one for progressives to adopt, but Lakoff's attempt at least identifies the problem.[21]

It's also instructive to see where liberals have failed at branding: President Clinton's New Covenant, for instance. That it is a lame phrase and so obviously derivative of both the New Deal and Kennedy's New Frontier didn't help, but the real reason Clinton's brand didn't work was because there was nothing behind it. There was no bold set of initiatives, only the cynical maneuverings of triangulation and compromise. The New Covenant didn't cohere and name a set of progressive policies; it was a replacement for them.

The fact that we must rely upon a sign at all may insult the sensibilities of traditional progressives who prefer some (impossible) unmediated real, but within a mass democracy linked by mass communication, progressives need to make their peace with representation. A progressive brand, conscientiously created, could give a cohesive sense of identity for ourselves as well as offer the quick and easy presentation necessary for mass-mediated identification and communication—that is, a thoughtful brand could help those within as well as those without discern exactly what is a progressive politics. Today, branding is a given. The real issue is who is doing it, us or them?

Advertising is a huge business. Nearly $250 billion was spent on ads in the United States alone in 2003; that is approximately, $850 for every man, woman, and child in this country.[22] But advertising, for all its immensity and importance, is in trouble. Print media sales are down, cable has lured audiences into commercial-free viewing, video and DVD rentals allow people to watch uninterrupted movies at home, channel changers encourage browsing . . . and then there is the bogeyman that strikes fear into every account manager's heart: TiVo. Ad spending declined in 2001 for the first time in four decades, and by the largest percentage since the Depression.[23] Traditional spaces for advertising are drying up and consumers are harder to reach.

But advertisers cannot afford to indulge in nostalgia, wishing for the good old days of the *Saturday Evening Post* and three channels of broadcast TV. Faced with necessity, advertisers have found new avenues into our psyche. Ads are now everywhere: on sidewalks, above urinals, and in schools. Facing both political and psychic resistance to old-style ads in new places, advertisers have found ways to integrate their message into our everyday lives: product placement in our entertainment and networks of "buzz agents" who turn everyday conversations into opportunities to hawk products. As veteran ad executive Carl Johnson explains, "It's almost accepted that the model is broken and it's time for a new approach . . . our last resort is an ad, if we can't think of anything else."[24]

Progressives are predictably—and justifiably—horrified by this totalitarian strategy of turning every space and every interaction into a sponsored moment. It is the death of the public sphere, the collapse of public space. All true, but it is also an opportunity to learn and adapt. Instead of bemoaning the eclipse of public discourse, why not reenergize it by moving politics outside of law courts and statehouses into the spaces and places of everyday life? Now that private shopping malls have replaced public town squares, our stock-in-trade speechifying and leaflet passing are limited anyway. We need to experiment with new ways to politicize space.

A fanciful example of this is the subway parties staged in New York City during the early 2000s. At a given time, at a given station, a large crowd assembles. When a train arrives we clamber aboard, covering advertisements with streamers and putting colored gels over the lights as the train turns into a party space. Sheena Bizarre, a participant, describes the scene:

There was a brass band on one side, and a boy with a boom box pumping techno on the other. We immediately started to dance around. I was given cups full of red wine. We smoked pot and smiled at one another. The city that has trained us to avoid contact and clutch our personals was now hosting the opposite. . . .

And then the first stop, ushering in New Yorkers who had no idea there could be a party on the MTA. The first passenger was a man in his fifties. He turned to me and said, "This is why I love New York." . . . I could only imagine this being a tourism commercial for the city. In my ideal world, it would be![25]

The function of the train party—besides being just pure, inexpensive fun—is to pose provocative questions about urban social relations and the proper use of a public service. Why is a Disneyfied Times Square and not people dancing in a subway car the public image of New York City? Why is it that paid advertisements instead of party streamers line the walls of subway cars? Through transforming a space and politicizing an environment, these questions aren't just asked, they are viscerally experienced.

The most valuable lesson progressives can learn from advertising, however, has to do with the power of desire. Advertising circumvents reason, working with the magical, the personal, and the associative. A journey of emotions rather than an argument of fact, its appeal is not cognitive, but primal. *Loyalty Beyond Reason*. This emotionality, perhaps all emotionality, disturbs progressives. As heirs to the Enlightenment, progressives have learned to privilege reason. Feelings are what motivate the others: Bible thumpers, consumers, terrorists, the mob. All true, but emotions also can motivate progressive politics. The problem is not desire, but where desire has been channeled.[26] The solution is not to abandon emotion with appeals to "reason" or "logic" or "fact," but to articulate desire differently: desire for a world in which fathers don't need to work so hard and can enjoy free and clean public spaces with their daughters, a desire for freedom and justice, a desire to win political power in order to pursue a progressive agenda.

The desire that is such a fecund environment for advertising can be the same passion that makes social change possible. In fact, one might argue that it is the failure of most mainstream politics to deliver on our political dreams that sets the stage for advertising's successes. John Berger, explaining the appeal of advertising, writes:

> The industrial society which has moved towards democracy and then stopped halfway is the ideal society for generating such an emotion [as social envy]. The pursuit of individual happiness has been acknowledged as a universal right. Yet the existing social conditions make the individual feel powerless. He lives in a contradiction between what he is and what he would like to be.[27]

Advertising capitalizes on these dreams deferred. Like Berger, progressives usually limit their attention to the negative desires that commercialism exploits, but it is important to recognize that Madison Avenue exalts more positive passions as well.

Advertising is not just about envy and fear; it is also about promise and plenty. In its own convoluted way, and for its own pecuniary objectives, Madison Avenue has been an invaluable propaganda bureau for progressive ideals, keeping hope alive.[28] Each advertisement, along with this or that product, sells the dream of a better life. The path to the realization of these dreams is certainly not to be found in the purchase of the products being sold, but we also can't get there by rejecting and distancing ourselves from the very desires mobilized by Madison Avenue. Progressives need to redirect these passions back to their original source: dissatisfaction with the world at hand and aspirations for a better one.

Progressive desire (as well as some rather more base ones) has provided material for copywriters and creative directors for decades. Now it is time to turn the tables. Advertising has provided us with sophisticated techniques to reach people and connect with their desires; now progressives need to use these tools to redirect progressive passions back into progressive politics. Nineteenth-century radicals once argued that only socialism could unlock the material promise of capitalism; today I believe that only progressive politics can free the fantasies trapped within advertising.

5. Recognize Everyone:
The Allure of Celebrity

A broad white beach spreads out on either side as you gaze out over the cool, blue water. You feel the warm sun blanket your body and glance down at your toned and tanned abdomen with pride. Returning to your lavishly decorated villa overlooking the ocean, you slip into designer clothes and enjoy a moonlit dinner of lobster and champagne. The next day you go shopping, driving your limited-production sports car into the city and entering stores where the sales staff eagerly serve you. You buy whatever you like. On the sidewalk outside people look at you and whisper. A bold one approaches and tells you how great you look and that they've always loved your work. That night you appear on national television, where you are asked for your opinions on love, creativity, and even world politics. The host nods his head thoughtfully, the audience applauds. A few more smiles for the photographers waiting outside, an artful wave of the hand, and you are driven up the coast to your home.

We know every detail of this life: what the beach looks like, how the house is decorated, the maximum speed of the sports car,

the clothes in the shops, and exactly how much all of it costs. We
know what it is like to be noticed and have our ideas listened to.
We know all this not because it is our life, but because it is the life
we watch celebrities live.

"We have yet to find out what will be the effect on morals and
religion and popular governance when the generation is in control which has had its main public experiences in the intermittent
blare of these sensations." It was 1927 when Walter Lippmann
wrote these words in an essay on celebrity and democracy in
Vanity Fair. Now that generations of us have lived lives of watching
stars live theirs, it is time to see if we can apprehend the meaning
of celebrity a bit more clearly, particularly its meaning for "popular governance."

Lippmann was pessimistic about the impact of celebrity culture
on democratic politics. With their attention turned to the stars,
he reasoned, people remained ignorant of the everyday workings
of life on terra firma: "It is no use trying to tell the public about
the Mississippi flood," he wrote, "when [celebrity murderer] Ruth
Snyder is on the stand."[1] The fact that the public was distracted
by celebrity instead of engaged in affairs of state was cited by an
increasingly conservative Lippmann as one more reason that politics was best left in the hands of an elite. Popular fascination with
the spectacle of celebrity was clear evidence of the public's lack of
interest in any sort of thoughtful, participatory politics.

And yet I, a salaried intellectual and seasoned activist, have
been known to while away the time in doctors' waiting rooms and
supermarket checkout lines pondering such subjects as "What
was Britney thinking?" when she got a boob job, made out with
Madonna on TV, married her hometown beau in Las Vegas, got
divorced the next day, married someone else, had a baby, . . . and
so on, ad infinitum.[2] Late at night, after student papers have been

graded, the final details of protests have been sorted, and the kids have been given their baths and are finally off to bed, I'm drawn like a moth to the blue glow of the E! channel, the stresses and strains of the day disappearing amid the chatter about my other family: the casts of *Friends*, *Scrubs*, and *CSI*.

I'm not the only one seduced by celebrity's siren song. Star watching is immensely popular and thus tremendously lucrative. *People* is the most profitable magazine in the United States, and the lives of the stars are detailed in scores of other magazines.[3] E! is the CNN of the stars with its 24/7 coverage of the entertainment industry, but nearly every television channel has at least one show devoted exclusively to celebrity. Then there are the ancillary industries: the products celebrities sponsor, the clothes they wear, the resorts they frequent, or the schools they attend that shine a little brighter and sell a little better thanks to the glow the stars cast upon them. (I taught an Olsen twin.) Even Lara Spencer, the informative hostess of public television's comfortably stodgy *Antiques Roadshow*, jumped ship to become the bubbly new face of *Entertainment Tonight*'s spin-off *The Insider*. Is nothing sacred?

While fame and hero worship have existed in one form or another for millennia (Leo Braudy, the academic chronicler of fame, pins the first star on Alexander the Great), modern media celebrity began in the first decades of the last century with the rise of Hollywood.[4] After experimenting with publicizing movies by story line and studio, it was discovered that what the public really responded to were actors. Stars were then manufactured by the studio system as meticulously as handcrafted luxury goods. Even great names like Buster Keaton were not exempt; his contract stipulated that he could not laugh in public. By 1910, *Photoplay*, the first magazine devoted exclusively to celebrities, was published, and by the 1930s Hollywood was the third-largest news source in the country, covered by some three hundred reporters, including one from the Vatican.[5]

As Lippmann understood, this mass appeal of celebrity has to be taken seriously in a mass democracy like our own. Since power (potentially) resides in the people, and the people are enamored with celebrity, it stands to reason that there are lessons to be learned here about democratic desire and how to speak to that desire. Since at least the presidency of John F. Kennedy, the celebrification of state affairs—staged photo-ops, emphasis on personalities, carefully crafted "behind-the-scenes" looks at candidates, the gossip and drama which take precedence over issues and policies—has become so commonplace in this country that the rest of the world merely refers to the whole process as the "Americanization" of politics.

There are nuances in how the relationship between politics and celebrity is understood and employed. The Democratic Party shamelessly links itself to Hollywood, trailing the stars around like mendicants pleading for money and media exposure. The radical left creates countercelebrities like Che Guevara, lies dormant while waiting for the next Great Leader, implodes with jealousy over the attention the current one has, and inevitably feels betrayed when its hero is turned into an icon to bolster a totalitarian state or sell Swatch watches. Meanwhile, progressive intellectuals retread Lippmann: celebrity culture is a phantasmagoric distraction from the real conditions affecting people. A circus without the bread. People simply need to turn off the TV, put down that magazine, and wake up to the real truth about their real lives.

The response to celebrity from the other end of the political spectrum has lately been, tactically speaking, more thoughtful. Consider the changing strategy of George W. Bush's public-image team. After brief and disastrous forays into star making—Top Gun W landing on the USS *Abraham Lincoln*, for instance—the White House began celebrating anticelebrity. Turning their client's deficiencies (and lack of popularity with the Hollywood crowd) to their advantage, they've repackaged Bush as Everyman, clearing brush on his ranch and stumbling over words at a press conference. Nowhere is this anticelebrity strategy more evident than in the Republican Party's beatification of the NASCAR dad: stereotyped as blue collar, beer drinking, and provincial. Would these guys ever stand a chance with a Hollywood starlet? No, but that's the point. These people, Republican Party people, are *real* people. Resentment of celebrity was always there, even in the celebrity media itself: the candid photo of the star with cellulite thighs or a bad facelift, the details on celebrity drug problems and rehab visits, and the catty commentary on the dresses worn on Oscar night, "When bad clothes happen to good people."[6] The Republican right neatly moved it into politics, stoking the envy which always accompanies desire. (The political genius of Ronald Reagan was that he could ride both sides. He could clear brush *and* fit in at the Academy Awards.)

The problem with each of these political responses to celebrity, from the anticelebrity of the Republican right to the procelebrity of the Democrats, through the countercelebrity of radicals to the just-say-no moralizing of the intellectuals, is that all are political responses to the epiphenomenon of celebrity itself. In other words, *they are a political response, not a political equivalent*, to celebrity. To move past reaction and toward replacement, we need to look at what comes before the stars and the hype—that is, pose the questions of what popular dreams does celebrity culture fulfill and how might these needs be otherwise addressed. Starting from this point we arrive at a different politics.[7]

So why is watching the media elite so popular with a mass audience? Part of the answer is addressed in the question itself: it is *because* the stars are an elite that they are so very popular. It is the very distance, and difference, of the stars lives from our own that makes them so fascinating. The medieval European peasant eating his meager porridge was once provided a vivid picture of heaven as a land of milk and honey; the world of celebrities offers us moderns a camera obscura image of the everyday world of flab, bills, and work in which we live. Revealing the "lifestyles of the rich and famous" is stock-in-trade for the celebrity media. Every magazine and TV show has its sections or segments on fabulous gala parties and the pricey designer gowns the stars wear to them. We are given tours of their palatial homes (or "cribs," in MTV's hipspeak) and peek into their garages at their luxury cars. We are treated to aerial views of the resorts that celebrities frequent and are provided with details about exactly how much it cost per night for Tom Cruise to rent the three-bedroom villa fronting the beach where he and his new love spent their holiday.[8] In the planet inhabited by celebrities, everyone is rich and beautiful and has time to revel in both.

But this netherworld doesn't only promise material plenty. It is also a land where women can dress as they like without being harassed, where sexual preferences are not an issue and racial distinction has been erased. Lesbian Ellen DeGeneres is covered in *Us*, but only for her new hairstyle, while *Celebrity Living* gushes over the wedding of (black) singer Seal and (white) model Heidi Klum, never mentioning their racial difference, only the celebrity status they share.[9] Even war appears as but an exotic backdrop to a USO tour by sexy pop singer Jessica Simpson and her (now ex-) husband and co-star Nick Lachey, the real *People* story being the state of their reality-televised marriage.[10] Celebrities live in paradise; we live in the real world. If this dream of heaven eludes us, we might as well watch someone else live it for us.[11]

In watching the stars live their blessed lives, however, we are also watching/imagining something else: ourselves being watched by others. Every fan wants to be a star. Celebrity was once obtainable only by the brave *and* noble born; in Homer's epics the Greek word for "hero" translates also as "gentleman" or "noble" and has clear class connotations.[12] But democracy and five hundred cable channels open up the dream of celebrity to everyone. As gay, short, rural-born, and later famous Andy Warhol prophesied: "In the future everyone will be famous for fifteen minutes." For every Paris Hilton, heir to a hotel fortune, there are thousands of small-town girls and farm boys ready to tell their stories of making it big. As any fan can tell you, Britney Spears grew up in rural Louisiana and is still a country girl at heart.

"Stars—they're just like us!" is a regular feature in Us magazine, reproducing grainy pictures taken through telephoto lenses of stars buying groceries, walking their dogs, or eating at Subway.[13] And *Life & Style* judges stars on whether they are a "Diva or Down-to-Earth."[14] Even a profile on Paris (no Hilton required; we're always on a first-name basis with the stars) in *Celebrity Living* insists that "friends say she'll always work," and then adds an even more common touch: "but when she's a mom, that will be her priority."[15] The European celebrity media may be more enamored with royalty, but even here they are at pains to present them as just folks—witness the late Diana, "The People's Princess." This emphasis on the humble roots and common touch of celebrities makes sense. No longer is it a learned scribe or royal court to which the celebrity owes his or her fame (or the industry its fortune), but to the regular people who watch the movies and TV shows, read the magazines, and buy the sponsored products.

The "humble roots and common tastes" celebrity stories not only make this contemporary Pantheon of the Gods acceptable to a democratic audience, but they also hold out the promise that this can happen to you. The impossible divide between the two worlds *can* be magically bridged. While the roots of reality TV lie in the economics of inexpensive programming, its popularity speaks to the desire to move from no one to someone, as this week's *Survivor* graces the cover of next week's celebrity glossy.

Even if you don't make it into the magazines, you can look like you do, and in a world of surfaces this is the next best thing. Two of the more recent entries into the celebrity magazine business, *Celebrity Living* and *Life & Style*, are devoted to giving their readers advice on how to get "The Look" of stars, providing the price and provenance of low-cost knockoffs of celebrity fashion, with $30 sandals from the Gap standing in for Kelly Ripa's $300 Jimmy Choo flip-flops.[16] You can be a star by buying (sort of) what stars buy; this is, after all, one of the primary ways we "know" them. But these palliatives for the fever to be famous are, like all consumer solutions, really self-perpetuating problems. Each move brings the fans back into the sight of a world they will never inhabit, and, thus dissatisfied, they start the cycle over again.

Progressive politics demands another solution: a break from the world of celebrity, not at the level of telling people to put down that magazine or not to buy that product, but in actually addressing the needs expressed by the popular desire to be famous. Some of this may be obvious, but it still bears repeating. What do celebrities have that we don't? They have wealth and they have leisure and they have beauty. Framed in terms of access instead of excess, these are bread-and-butter issues for progressives: better pay, shorter workweeks, mandatory vacation time, and universal health and dental care.[17]

But above all, stars are *seen*. Everywhere they go, from the Academy Awards to shopping at the mall, they are spotted, photographed, and broadcast. In a word, they *appear*. Heroes of the past were known for what they did: conquering nations, inventing contraptions, or flying across oceans or into space. The best remembered of these heroes imbued their acts with cultural meaning and made sure someone was around to record them, yet it is still their acts that made them famous.[18] The modern-day media icons are known, as historian Daniel Boorstin has put it, "primarily for their well-knownness."[19] They are famous for being famous.

Within our present economy of signs, celebrities have currency. They exist. We, on the other hand, do not. We may appear before our loved ones, neighbors, and co-workers, but in the realm of the public image we are invisible. How often and in what form do most citizens appear before a mass public? Maybe for a few seconds on the nightly news when tragedy befalls us, in a blur on the Jumbotron when the camera pans past us in the crowd, or as a disembodied statistic in an opinion poll. That's all. We are the watchers, not the watched. And, as the nameless protagonist of Ralph Ellison's *Invisible Man* understood, there is no pain, no indignity worse than invisibility. The fantasy of celebrity, above all, speaks to the desire to be visible.

Progressives have responded to this call before. When New Deal agencies like the Farm Security Administration commissioned photographs of "nobodies," like the Dust Bowl migrants memorialized in Dorothea Lange's haunting portraits, they were visually reconstituting what it meant to be an American after two decades of photographic saturation of "somebodies" like Rudolph Valentino and Palm Beach socialites. They were taking seriously the modern desire of all of us to be seen. Likewise, the murals sponsored by the Works Progress Administration retold history not just as a story of great things done by great men, but as an accomplishment of everyday citizens. On the walls of post offices and public buildings across the United States, publicly funded artists sketched out past, present, and future fantasies of a world where the experience of ordinary men and women was recognized and their work rewarded, creating a counterspectacle to that of extraordinary celebrity.[20] The progressive administrators of the New Deal didn't try to deny these dreams; instead they provided the vision to reimagine them.

In our mass-mediated world the fantasy of being seen is most often thought of literally: to be an image on TV or in a magazine or on the silver screen. Making this dream a reality today is technically possible in ways unimaginable only a generation ago. Community television, Internet blogs, low-wattage radio transmitters, camera phones, photocopied zines, and so forth have democratized our ability to appear as a mediated image or voice. Certainly progressives should encourage these things by making the case for more community TV channels with better studios and technical training, free Internet access and Web hosting for everyone, legalized microradio, and so on. Any progressive political program must include policies that provide affordable or free access to media for popular expression. But the will to visibility speaks to something larger.

What does it really mean to be seen? It means to be *recognized*. This is the more important challenge: how can progressives create a politics that recognizes everyone? The anticorporate globalization movement may offer a clue. To call this movement a movement, however, is really a misnomer. As *No Logo*'s Naomi Klein and others have described, it is really a "movement of movements." This movement of movements is not composed of large organizations with star leaders—even if the media exalt one or two to that status. Instead it is made up of tens of thousands of little groups. "It is tempting to pretend that someone did dream up a master plan for mobilization in Seattle," Klein writes about the anti–World Trade Organization protest in 1999 that brought this movement of movements to the world's attention. "But I think it was much more a matter of large-scale coincidence. A lot of smaller groups organized to get themselves there and then found to their surprise just how broad and diverse a coalition they had become a part of."[21]

The size of these groups is critical. They are intimate affairs, small enough for each participant to have an active role in shaping the group's direction and voice. They may come together for a mass protest or gather for a global forum, but most discussions and decisions take place at a very local level. In these "affinity groups," as they are called, every person is recognized: in short, they exist. (The right, organizing through churches, has accomplished much the same thing.)

It was as a member of just such an affinity group that I traveled down to the protests against the 2000 International Monetary Fund and World Bank meetings in Washington, D.C. Before we left New York we met as a group, a fairly large group, but still small enough to draw together in a circle in a big room. Through a series of meetings held in an old community center we discussed the politics and economics of the IMF and World Bank, the purpose of the mass protest, and how we, as a group, could be the most useful to the overall goal of drawing attention to these institutions. (We decided to dress up as sharks in tuxedoes and form kick lines in the street while belting out our version of "Mack the Knife"—loan sharks, get it?) In the process of these affinity-group meetings we got to know each other: our strengths and weaknesses, our fears and hopes, our politics. We also learned how to work together.

This intimate knowledge was critical when we finally made it to D.C. where, amid the swirling chaos of a mass protest, the best-laid plans—as usual—were rendered useless. Since we all recognized one another we were able to stick together on the street, even when charged by riot police or surrounded by Maoist extremists. As a small group we could huddle together on a moment's notice, discuss the situation we were in, and improvise and change our tactics on the fly. Recognizing each other's goals and limits we could plan a course of action that was acceptable to everyone. What could have been alienating, bewildering, and quite frightening was instead an empowering experience. We even managed to block a bus full of IMF delegates, and get a little press, with our choreographed kick line.

The mainstream models of progressive politics, from the professionalized Democratic Party to the ritualistic "March on Washington" of those further to the left, don't learn from celebrity culture; they ape it. A star up on the platform is seen and heard, while the rest of us merely watch, applauding at the right moments. This has to change. Instead of waiting for the charismatic camera-ready politician to arrive and save the party, and in place of organizing demonstrations around star speakers, we need to look downward, concentrating on building local organizations where all participants can witness the efficacy of their participation and, in turn, have their participation witnessed by others.[22] The scream of the angry revolutionary who cries, "I am nothing and I should be everything" resides, mute, within every celebrity watcher.[23] Progressives must cultivate a process of politics where people, at the very least, are "something." Unless we acknowledge and respond to this aspiration of visibility, progressive politics will remain equally invisible.

Celebrity also taps into another popular desire: our wish to know, to discuss what we know, and then make meaning from it. Or, in terms less exalted, celebrity culture feeds our love of gossip. Our society is made up of people from different backgrounds and drawn from different places; we are scattered geographically and move frequently. Because of this we don't share a common set of characters to talk about . . . except celebrities. The conversations and speculation that might have once taken place around the village well or after church about this or that member of the community now borrow their source material from *People* magazine. Celebrity gossip, like gossip throughout time, works as a public stage on which to play out and judge behavior and values. As I write this chapter the buzz is over the love triangle of Jen, Brad, and Angelina. To fill in the uninitiated: Jennifer Aniston, one of the stars of the TV hit *Friends*, was married to Brad Pitt, movie star and general hunk. Jen and Brad recently divorced, amid rumors that Brad wanted to raise a family while Jen wanted to continue working on her career. Enter Angelina Jolie, the tattooed movie starlet best known for her charitable work fighting poverty in the Third World, who courted the still-married Brad on the movie set of their co-starred blockbuster.

This is the stuff that sells magazines. Over a split picture of Angelina and Jen, *In Touch* splashes the headline: "Angelina buys Brad a ring. NOW IT'S WAR! Jen fights back with a sexy make-over."[24] It is also the stuff that provides grist for the moral mill. Article after article and conversation after conversation about these three celebrities touches upon questions germane to us all: Was Jen right to put her career before family? Was Brad justified in leaving his wife because of this? Do Angelina's public good works make up for her private transgressions? In the absence of a unifying moral textbook, celebrity gossip becomes one of the places where we work out what is right and what is wrong and, through our interpretations of the actions of these characters, eke out a moral code to live by.

To share in the gossip you must know the Byzantine intricacies of this world, and the celebrity industry encourages this expertise and attendant judgment. Read enough celebrity magazines and watch enough entertainment specials and you will have amassed an immense amount of knowledge on such trivial subjects as the population of Renée Zellweger's hometown of Katy, Texas (11,755, in case you are wondering).[25] Because the world of celebrity is so distant from our own we become part of it not by acting within it but by being, as a regular feature in In Touch magazine promises, "In the Know."[26]

But there is always more to know. In Star, body language "experts" interpret paparazzi photos as carefully as high priestesses once consulted entrails.[27] Inside TV is full of "secrets" revealed to their readers: "Patrick's Secret Passion" (race cars) and "Secrets of Rob and Amber's Romantic Wedding" (none that I could discern).[28] All secrets are, of course, helpfully provided by the star's public relations agent. And because at some level we know this, we also want to know the story about the story: the real deal on this imaginary universe. Exposés on the mechanics of star manufacture have been part of the discourse of celebrity watching since its modern beginnings. The first story exposing the machinery behind the making of celebrities was published in Collier's in 1920, only ten years after the first celebrity magazine appeared.[29] Alongside the will to ignorance that Lippmann thought revealed itself in our infatuation with celebrities is our desire to know.

The pleasure we derive in knowing everything about something, even if this something is really nothing, might best be understood by considering the expertise expected in the rest of one's life. As Lippmann argued more than seventy-five years ago, the complexities of modern law, politics, science—even the variable interest rate on our credit cards—are so daunting that it takes a lifetime of study to render meaningful judgment in just one field. This specialization of knowledge has left the majority of us ignorant and mute about the very things that should matter the most to us: our political and legal systems, the environment or the economy.

Expertise is also not encouraged in the work many of us do for a living. According to the Bureau of Labor Statistics, retail sales and cashiers are the number-one and -two employment categories in the United States.[30] How much does one have to know to sell a shirt at the Gap or ring up a sale at Wal-Mart? Knowing a lot about something like the world of celebrity gives us the pleasure and power of being an expert in a world where popular expertise is not needed or solicited.

The pleasures of popular knowledge need to be addressed politically. *Scientia est Potentia*—knowledge is power—as every school child has had drilled into his head. But this is nothing more than another empty Enlightenment adage if the path between knowledge and power is impassable. As things stand today, it is probably true that you need a law degree and a doctorate in international relations to make sense of a global trade agreement. But this doesn't have to be. While there will always be a need for specialized knowledge, complex issues can be presented in such a way that they can be mastered by ordinary citizens.

During the Great Depression, President Franklin D. Roosevelt broadcast regular "fireside chats" on the radio. This was part of the creation and dissemination of FDR's public persona, recasting this American aristocrat as a plain-talking friend, speaking intimately to the common man from the living room radio. It was propaganda, scripted by his policy advisers and stylized by the playwright Robert Sherwood. But it was not empty propaganda, for these fireside chats had real content. In his first address, on March 12, 1933, a week after his inauguration and in the midst of a monumental banking crisis, Roosevelt spoke to the nation in a patient, personal voice. "My friends," he began,

> I want to talk for a few minutes with the people of the United States about banking—to talk with the comparatively few who understand the mechanics of banking, but more particularly with the overwhelming majority of you who use banks for the making of deposits and drawing of checks. I want to tell you what has been done in the last few days, and why it was done, and what the next steps are going to be.

Which is exactly what FDR did, explaining to the population how the banking system worked:

> First of all, let me state the simple fact that when you deposit money in a bank the bank does not put money into a safe deposit vault. It invests your money in many different forms of credit—in bonds, in commercial paper, in mortgages and in many other kinds of loans. In other words, the bank puts your money to work to keep the wheels of industry and agriculture turning round. A comparatively small part of the money that you put into the bank is kept in currency—an amount which in normal times is wholly sufficient to cover the cash needs of the average citizen. In other words, the total amount of all currency in the country is only a comparatively small proportion of total deposits in all the banks of the country.[31]

Roosevelt continued, describing why the system had failed with a run on the banks and then what the government planned to do about it: temporarily closing the nation's banks, and reorganizing, regulating, and insuring the banking industry.

Thirty times during his presidency FDR engaged the public with often highly technical subjects explained in nontechnical—but not simplistic—language. FDR's fireside chats were not streams of disembodied facts and figures but facts and figures woven into narratives that spoke to people's everyday lives. The integration of information into personal narrative is also a prime technique of celebrity culture, but in place of pseudo-facts of the stars' ether existence, Roosevelt (and his speechwriters) spun out stories about drought, the judiciary, mortgages, unions, currency, the programs of the New Deal, and, later in his administration, foreign policy and war. FDR put Lippmann's pessimism about the capacity of citizens to know and reason to the test by opening up the opportunity for people to amass knowledge and render judgment on issues and policies that affected their lives. As public relations historian Stuart Ewen describes: "Unspoken, but evident, was a determined and unaccustomed faith in ordinary people's ability to make sense of things."[32]

Recent presidents have carried on Roosevelt's tradition of the weekly radio address, but the content-rich formula of the fireside chats has given way to the empty rhetorical sound bite. Here are the first words of George W. Bush's 2004 Labor Day radio address on "The Economy":

> Good morning. America is the home to the most dedicated, innovative, and decent workers in the world. And thanks to their effort and enterprise, America's economy is strong and growing stronger.[33]

The contrast is striking: instead of a patient explication of the economy and explanation of the challenges Americans face, we are treated to boosterism: everything is great, don't worry about anything, God Bless America. As with the world of celebrity, an idealized portrait is presented for our admiration and identification.

But does it have to be this way? The historical example of FDR's fireside chats, along with the continuing popular interest in, understanding of, and debate regarding all things celebrity, suggests that there may be a will (if not yet a way) for a public intellectual engagement with politics. It's not that people don't like facts; it's that most of us like our facts made accessible, meaningful, and personal. Celebrity culture provides this with its banalities about the lives of the stars. Our challenge is to present the knowledge necessary for an informed citizenry in a way that resonates with people's *own* lives.

But it is important to recognize that people's lives don't just revolve around political issues like banking regulation, the state of the judiciary, and the right to unionize. Our lives are also composed of dreams and desires, which, to the progressive mind, might sometimes seem trivial, irrational, or politically incorrect. The goal in progressive communications should not be to speak to one side or the other but to combine the real and the fantastic, the weighty and the light, and the political and the personal in the same way they are all mixed up in people's hearts, minds, and lives.

This is what *BUST* does. Begun in 1993 by Debbie Stoller as a homemade photocopied zine, it is now a slick, professional, and profitable magazine with a circulation of 81,000 and a fiercely loyal readership.[34] *BUST* is a feminist magazine and makes no apologies for its politics, but the "feminist" it addresses through its articles has an impressively varied—read: normal—set of interests. In the June/July 2005 issue, for instance, there is an essay about a worker's organization in Cleveland that advocates for jobs for blue-collar women. But a couple of pages following this article on "Hard-Hatted Women" and gendered income inequity is a feature on the history of rouge; a few pages before it is a profile of pop singer Aimee Mann. Elsewhere in the issue are a report on the erosion of women's rights in Iraq under the U.S. occupation, a photo fashion spread, an article on war-related rape in the Democratic Republic of Congo, directions for styling a French twist hairdo, a piece on female long-distance truck drivers, an interview with movie starlet Sandra Oh, recipes for Southern road food, a feminist critique of weight-loss programs, a report on abortion records seized by the conservative attorney general of Kansas, and tips on shopping for shoes. In BUST, politics is packaged as part of a panoply of women's passions, on par with celebrity and fashion.[35] It's all part of what Stoller calls "an alternative, embraceable women's culture."

"So much of women's culture," she explains, "is about denial and restrictiveness; diets and directions on how to please your man." Traditional feminist media merely flips this formula over. "Instead of supermodels they offer up 'positive' role models" of superfeminists, and in response to articles on the search for the perfect husband they provide "lists of bad things that men do to women." BUST strives to provide something different, emphasizing pleasure rather than denial. (At staff meetings Stoller warns her editors against "too much leafy green vegetables"—content that's good for you but not much fun to swallow.[36]) The result is a magazine that recognizes the complicated lives and dreams of its readership and makes sure to speak to a wide range of women's passions. And I really do mean a wide range. BUST might broach issues of gender inequality and foreign policy, but every issue concludes with a "one-handed read" of erotica. With her magazine Stoller reframes both "feminism" and "women's culture," including what some might consider trivial pursuits in the former and what others might see as bummer politics in the latter. BUST opens up the definitions in both cases, making room to include more passions and—critical for a democratic politics—more people.

We live in an age where spectacles make us stupid; we can engineer them to make us smarter. The national question of "What was Britney thinking?" might be replaced with "What could I be thinking?" (and talking and doing) about social security, about foreign policy, about democracy, but only if progressives learn to speak a political language and devise political policies which resonate with the wide range of human desires, including those currently manifested within celebrity culture. The wish to be recognized and the will to know don't need to be addressed solely through celebrity. Considered from a different angle and moved into a political realm, these desires can serve as the driving forces behind an engaged and informed citizenry. In answer to Walter Lippmann's initial question, the result of generations exposed to the "blare of these sensations" might be not just the sublimation, but also the cultivation of the very ingredients necessary for "popular governance."

Before we charge the barricades waving a copy of People in the air and rush to actualize the political equivalent to celebrity, a warning is in order. Popular attraction to the fantasies of celebrity points up a troubling popular fantasy: life without consequence. Think back to gossip. When we gossip about people close to us, in the backs of our minds lingers the fear that what we've said will come back and haunt us. We wake the next morning with a moral hangover at having trashed our friends the night before. Engaging in celebrity gossip engenders none of this. No matter what nasty, catty things I say about Brad, Jen, and Angelina, the words will never reach their ears. We live in separate worlds and communication flows one way.[37]

This disengagement operates at a more profound level as well. The fascination with celebrities is an escape, not only into a fantasy of luxury and leisure as I discussed earlier, but into "activity" with no agency. Just as the lives of the Greek gods on Mount Olympus or the whims of the capricious Old Testament God of the Book of Job were outside the reach of mortal actions, it is not within our power to determine whether Brad ends up with Angelina or goes back to Jen. Jessica and Nick divorced, despite the 64 percent of their fans recorded in an *In Touch* reader's poll who felt they shouldn't.[38] It is not within our power to determine *anything* in their world (except their popularity by withholding our worship). For all the illusions of closeness created by insider knowledge and behind-the-scenes looks, for all our dreams of living their dream, we also know that celebrity is forever distant. Within their world what can I build? Nothing. What can I destroy? Nothing. What can I change? Nothing. It is a world, after all, I can *only* experience vicariously. Through celebrities I can fulfill my desires to live another life, a life perhaps more exciting and adventurous than my own, but there is no risk. I am safe. Doubly safe, because unlike the gods of old who could give us boils or flood our lands, celebrities have no real power over us either. It's a common critique that following the lives of celebrities is a waste of time. Perhaps it is, but what I'm really worried about is that it is a squandering of our subjectivity. Sound and fury, signifying nothing.

Sociologist Joshua Gamson, in his book *Claims to Fame*, argues that celebrity culture is best understood by looking at it as a game. Not a game of open, engaged, and transformative play, as discussed in a previous chapter, but a game in the sense that nothing really matters. For years it has been rumored that Tom Cruise is gay. Is he? A true believer would insist he is not, pointing to the stories about his tropical trysts and well-publicized romance with Katie Holmes. The cynic might insist that these are public-relations covers for his homosexuality. But most of us like to play the game. Why, in high school, did Tom study for the priesthood and then join the wrestling team? Why did Tom have only adopted children with previous wives? Why did Tom and Katie's vacation villa have multiple bedrooms? Why is he *soooo* publicly enthusiastic about his new romance? Truth is not the issue; it is the ongoing guessing game—which can never be resolved—that is the purpose and the pleasure of celebrity culture. As Gamson writes, "Celebrity watchers continually *ride* the belief/disbelief and fiction/reality axes."[39]

Is this so different than how we've learned to approach public affairs as well? Faced with an informational economy that floods us with facts and truths, and a political system which discourages input, the adaptive response is to neither believe or disbelieve but to stay above it all, seeing it as some sort of a game that we can never really know, and certainly not affect, so we might as well enjoy the ride. As an activity without consequence, where participation is vicarious and pleasure is found in the form of a no-stakes game, celebrity culture can be understood as an escape from democracy with its attendant demands for responsibility and participation.[40]

This is the primary problem facing progressives: people need to *want* political agency in order to live the dream they now just watch. It may be, however, that celebrity points to the opposite: the popular desire to disengage from consequential activity. Instead of realizing paradise here, perhaps we prefer to fantasize about a fantasy, investing our energy in an insubstantial counterworld in the clouds while our everyday life sinks lower and lower.

There is a politics that discourages democratic engagement yet speaks persuasively to the desire of people to live within and through fantasy. Such a political system, the German critic Walter Benjamin argued in 1937, gives people aesthetic identification and enjoyment in place of political and economic power.[41] He was, of course, referring to fascism. But we don't have to go there. Maybe, just maybe, we invest so much in celebrity because we see in their world glimmers of the world in which we'd like to live, and given a political model that speaks to our dreams, we just might act to bring it about.

6. Imagine an Ethical Spectacle

When imagining what an ethical spectacle might look like it is hard to overlook the two elephants in the room. Frolicking Aryans, ordered marches, adulation of the Führer, and other scenes from *Triumph of the Will* flash in front of your eyes; jingles of a thousand and one advertisements ring in your ears. Fascism and commercialism appear to have cornered the market on the political use of fantasy and the mobilization of desire. At first glance the spectacle engineered and employed by these two seem quite different, operating according to dissimilar principles. Fascist spectacle is overtly political and inherently collective. The ideal conjured up is one of mass obedience and a sacrifice of the individual to a higher will. Commercial spectacle is economic and individualistic. The promise it makes is of singular specialness and individual transformation. Yet both fascism and commercialism share core characteristics of spectacle: looking beyond reason, rationality, and self-evident truth and making use of story, myth, fantasy, and imagination to further their respective agendas. Both meet people where they are, draw upon preexisting desires, then redirect them. As unsettling as it may first seem, these are also the central features of an ethical spectacle.

To speak of ethics, codes of right and good conduct, when considering the horror of fascism or the banality of commercialism seems sacrilegious. Given the unsavory nature of these twin beasts, how can spectacle ever be considered ethical? The answer is simple . . . and not. All spectacle, no matter how horrifying or banal, can be ethical. What is at issue is what or whose ethics are being expressed. The Nuremburg rally of 1934 captured on film by Leni Riefenstahl masterfully articulated the ethics of the Nazi Party: order, discipline, obedience, the glorification of the Volk, and the exclusion of the Other. By Nazi standards, the spectacle was ethical. Likewise, guided by ethics of market freedom and the desirability of profitability, an advertisement that appeals to an individual's desire and channels that desire into consumption is ethical. Consumer sovereignty is a different sort of "will of the people," but no more or less ethical than that expressed through a fascist rally.

The bogeymen of Nazi propaganda and consumer advertising have long been used to limit progressive thinking about the possible uses of spectacle. The threats are ever-present: "Be careful or you'll end up reproducing the Third Reich" or "It's a slippery slope toward treating citizens as consumers." But is there really a chance of this happening given who we are, where we are, and what we believe? These cautions serve more as censors of creative thought than real concerns to be heeded. The fact that progressives worry about abusing power before we have any is less a sign of our concern for the responsibility that comes with power than it is a symptom of our reluctance to really pursue it.[1] Our real concern should be what set of ethical precepts structures *our* spectacle. Here's a place to start.

Progressives believe in democracy. This includes universal suffrage in a representational government, but it also encompasses the expansion of more direct and participatory forms of democracy. We hold that all people are created equal. However, we also believe that equality, in opportunity if not eventual outcome, has to be guaranteed throughout a person's life and into future generations. This means that hierarchies of privilege must be continually undermined.

Progressives believe that life is interconnected and interdependent. As such we are responsible for our neighbors, as they are responsible for us; we care for the earth, as it cares for us: we are a global community. But the community that progressives value is not a homogeneous one. We believe that there is intrinsic value in individual expression and that the collective is made stronger and more vibrant through the inclusion of and discussion among many differing voices.

And while it may seem paradoxical to raise this in a book exalting dreams and spectacle, it needs to be acknowledged that part of the progressive tradition, from Enlightenment empiricists through Marxist materialists to welfare state liberals, is a strong belief in the essentiality of the real. However complicated this relationship might be, progressives believe that there is truth and falsehood, and that an honest politics must acknowledge and engage the real conditions of the world. And finally, and simply, we believe in progress: the future can be better than the present.

In brief, then, a *progressive* ethical spectacle will be one that is directly democratic, breaks down hierarchies, fosters community, allows for diversity, and engages with reality while asking what new realities might be possible. These standards are few and broad—and rather empty at this level of abstraction. They are not exhaustive, but they are also not as exhausting as the usual laundry list of left-liberal ideals. Whatever their limitations, they provide a set of principles to organize the observations of the previous chapters and guide our imaginings of what an ethical spectacle might look like.

Participatory Spectacle

All spectacle counts on popular participation. The fascist rallies in Japan, Italy, and Germany; the military parades through Moscow's Red Square; the halftime shows at the Super Bowl—all demand an audience to march, stand, or do the wave. Even the more individualistic spectacle of advertising depends upon the distant participation of the spectator, who must become a consumer. But the public in both fascist and commercial spectacles only participates from the outside, as a set piece on a stage imagined and directed by someone else. As Siegfried Kracauer, a German film critic writing in the 1920s about "the mass ornament," the public spectacles that prefigured Nazi rallies, observed, "Although the masses give rise to the ornament, they are not involved in thinking it through."[2]

Ethical spectacle demands a different sort of participation. The people who participate in the performance of the spectacle must also contribute to its construction. As opposed to the spectacles of commercialism and fascism, the public in an ethical spectacle is not considered a stage prop, but a co-producer and co-director. This is nothing radical, merely the application of democratic principles to the spectacles that govern our lives. If it is reasonable to demand that we have a say in how our schools are run or who is elected president, why shouldn't we have the right to participate in the planning and carrying out of spectacle?

This is what we did with Reclaim the Streets in New York City.

The planning meetings for our events were open to all (even to a few undercover police officers for a time) and we encouraged everyone to take part in the protests' construction, breaking into a number of smaller working groups (logistics, legal, media, sound, props, outreach) so that every individual's mind and hands were engaged. Then, on the day of the party/protest, we encouraged further involvement by making space for whatever sorts of contributions the participants wanted to bring. Fire-breathers would show up, or a marching band, or radical cheerleaders. It personalized the protest so that it spoke to and of its participants, engaging them and reveling in their diverse contributions. A potluck protest.

A more mainstream—and larger-scale—example of this sort of spectacular participation happens every Sunday in the megachurches that have sprouted up across the United States in recent years. A few years back I accompanied my sister-in-law's family to one such church. They live in Orange County, California, and their "local" house of worship is Saddleback Church, a massive institution built and presided over by the Reverend Rick Warren. We drove into a parking lot the size of a football field and walked into a church as big as an airplane hangar. Inside were thousands of people. Reverend Warren bounded out on stage to the beat of a live rock band. Lit by racks of theatrical lights, his face simultaneously telecast on massive screens overhead, he launched into his sermon. It wasn't my kind of Christianity. I prefer my religious spectacle with Latin and incense, and this was more upbeat and Oprah, but there was no denying the feeling of community and sense of energy in that immense room.

Each week Warren preaches to twenty thousand people at his church. How does this huge flock engage as individuals in the spectacle he performs? The same way that leftist protesters (and

Islamic terrorists) do: through small affinity groups. Saddleback might serve tens of thousands of people at a time, but many of those people are connected to the church at a much more intimate level, through small groups meeting regularly for Bible study, charity work, or just to socialize with other Christians. This approach is not peculiar to Saddleback Church: nearly 40 million Americans are in some sort of religious affinity group scaled for intimacy.[3] While the congregation of Saddleback is not directly involved in the scripting of the spectacle that Reverend Warren performs each weekend, the sense of belonging they have has everything to do with the individual participation they have in the life of the church and in each other's lives throughout the rest of the week. It may not be the direct participation of the activists of Reclaim the Streets, but it is a model that breaks down the director/directed dichotomy.

A participatory spectacle is not a spontaneous one; an organizer (or a minister) needs to set the stage for participation to happen. But the mission of the organizer of an ethical spectacle differs from that of other spectacles. She has her eyes on two things. First is the overall look of the spectacle—that is, the desires being expressed, the dreams being displayed, the outcome being hoped for. In this way her job is the same as the fascist propagandist or the Madison Avenue creative director. But then she has another job. She must create a situation in which popular participation not only *can* happen but *must* happen for the spectacle to come to fruition.

The theorist/activists of the Situationists made a useful distinction between spectacle and situation. The spectacle they condemned as a site of "nonintervention"; there was simply no space for a spectator to intervene in what he or she was watching because it demanded only passivity and acquiescence. The

Situationists saw it as their mission to fight against "the society of the spectacle," but they also felt a responsibility to set something else in motion to replace it. "We must try and construct situations," their master theorist Guy Debord wrote in 1957. These "situations" were no less staged events than fascist rallies, but their goal was different. The Situationists encouraged people to *dérive*—drift through unfamiliar city streets—and they showed mass culture films after "detourning" the dialogue, dubbing the actor's lines to comment upon (or make nonsense of) the film being shown and the commercial culture from which it came. These situations, it was hoped, would create "collective ambiances," which encouraged participants to break out of the soporific routine of the society of the spectacle and participate in the situation unfolding around them: to make sense of new streets and sights, look at celluloid images in a new and different way, and thereby alter people's relationship to their material and media environment.[4] As Debord wrote: "The role played by a passive or merely bit-playing 'public' must constantly diminish, while that played by those who cannot be called actors but rather, in a new sense of the term, 'livers,' must steadily increase." Whereas actors play out a tight script written by another, "livers" write their own script through their actions within a given setting. The ideal of the "situation" was to set the stage for "transformative action."[5]

I don't find the semantic distinction between the words *situation* and *spectacle* all that helpful, but the distinction between nonintervention and transformative action is useful. What a good organizer of ethical spectacles must do is provide plenty of opportunity for intervention at an intimate and personal level, for only this will translate into some sort of action that is transformative to both the individual actor and, ideally, the larger society—that is, they must set the stage for what video game designers call "transformative play."[6]

Simply spectating should not be summarily dismissed. There is a great deal of pleasure derived in just watching—taking in what others have created for us, being drawn along into a tale told by others—and it needs to be acknowledged and addressed. If there is no ethical form of spectatorship, we'll lose those people—and the part of all of us—who sometimes prefer just to watch. If the opportunity to watch is not provided within the ethical spectacle, we'll turn elsewhere for those pleasures, and again progressive politics will be equated with denial and sacrifice.

While liberals and those on the left are often branded (with some good reason) as sour and serious, there is also a counter-tradition of progressive politics that is very much about joking. Consider, for example, Jonathan Swift's 1729 "modest proposal" to solve the problem of the poor in Ireland by eating them. Think of the Yippies' call to levitate the Pentagon in 1967. There's the mocking performance of plutocracy by the Billionaires for Bush and the Situationists' detourned movies, or Jon Stewart's sardonic take on politics on the *Daily Show* and its spin-off, *The Colbert Report*, an ironic send-up of conservative media punditry. In all these progressive narratives, satire, irony, camp, and humor are integral. Not only does this make the message more palatable and thus popular, it also makes political sense in another way.

Jokes are active, social things. More than any other form of communication they demand participation from their audience. Meaning in a joke is incomplete; not all information is given, and the remaining part must be provided by the recipient. This is why it is possible to not "get" a joke. When the humor is satire or irony, as in the case of Swift's essay, the Billionaires' shtick, or in

much of Stewart and Colbert's humor, the sense of shared meaning is even more intense. Given clues to what the author or performer *doesn't* think, the spectator deciphering an ironic text has
to use his or her imagination to figure out what the creator *does*
believe. The spectator helps create the message by providing its
incomplete negation.[7] As such, jokes create a sort of interdependency. When we watch a stand-up comic bomb on stage, we
are witnessing the rejection of a social bond; that's why it is so
excruciatingly painful. But it is also what is so magical about
comedy when it works, for the audience and the comic create
something together. Good humor confers an instant intimacy between the comic and the audience, both of whom share in the
meaning-making.

This narrative interdependency works against hierarchy. The
Nazis, for instance, were unabashedly elitist in their creation of
spectacular meaning. In *Mein Kampf* Adolf Hitler wrote, "The re-
ceptivity of the great masses is very limited, their intelligence
is small, but their power of forgetting is enormous."[8] This is not
a philosophy which considers the audience as collaborators in
meaning-making; it is a top-down model that assumes an active
producer and a rather dim receiver. (Nazis were not known for
their great sense of humor, either.) Ethical spectacle turns this
model of communication and power on its head.

The demonstrators who shut down the city of London in 1998
called their protest a "Carnival against Capitalism," and many of
the large street protests over the past decade could be described
as carnivalesque. Accompanying the more traditional march-
and-chanters, protesters also form samba bands, shimmy in the
streets, don clown makeup, and, in the case of anti–Free Trade
Agreement protests in Quebec in 2001, erect a medieval catapult
to hurl stuffed animals over the barrier set up to keep demonstra-

tors away from bankers and bureaucrats. These protests embody the carnival in spirit as well as form. Carnival is a form of popular culture that levels hierarchies and demands participation, argues the literary critic Mikhail Bakhtin in his book on the medieval humorist Rabelais. "Carnival is not a spectacle seen by the people," Bakhtin claims. "They live in it, and everyone participates because its very idea embraces all the people."[9] It's not a circus staged for an audience but a collective gathering where the world is—temporarily—turned upside down.

Not all politics are suitable for joking. After the terrorist attacks on 9/11, Reclaim the Streets in New York called a temporary moratorium on our street carnivals and theatrical hijinks. We continued with our participatory style of organizing protests, but it was inappropriate to clown with the smell of death still in the air and laugh at the warmongering going on in the White House. But to dwell on humor misses the point. Humor is just *one* way that politicos have figured out how to create a spectacle that engages people, making them into active participants ("livers") even in the very spectacles they enjoy just watching.

Spectacle, by tradition, is antidemocratic. It is created by the few to be followed by the many, and while it can make the promise of inclusion (into *das Volk* or a consumer market) it actually reinforces the reality of hierarchy. The "participation" it encourages is a tightly choreographed sham. There are some who direct and others (most of us) who are directed. It doesn't have to be this way. By insisting on popular participation in both the production and consumption of the spectacle, we can transform a political and aesthetic form used to control and channel popular desire into one that can express it. With the active engagement of its participants, a progressive spectacle becomes a place where hierarchies of creator and spectator, producer and consumer, leader and follower are broken down. With a democratized spectacle there is no man behind the curtain, pulling the levers to create the illusions and bellowing into a microphone: "I am Oz." Participatory spectacle puts us all behind the curtain, a community of creator/spectators, and the curtain disappears.

Open Spectacle

The Nazis may have propagandized a mass politics with "no spectators, only actors," but in their practice their "actors" were only so in the theatrical sense: scripted players in a larger spectacle, given their lines and cues within a drama written out in advance by a party elite.[10] Even before the Nazi rise to power, Rudolf Hess, an intimate of Hitler who transcribed and edited *Mein Kampf*, theorized "that the Führer must be absolute in his propaganda speeches . . . he must never leave his listeners the freedom to think something else is right."[11] The spectacle of commercial culture uses different techniques but ultimately has the same goal. A good advertisement, for example, doesn't tell you what to buy, but it raises questions for which the only possible answer is the purchase of the product. A halftime show at the Super Bowl may not seem to have an overt message or a desired response on the part of the audience (other than to keep us watching so that the network can charge millions of dollars a second for the interspersed advertisements), but the entertainment is scripted in such a way that there is no chance to explore. The contrived "wardrobe malfunction" exposing Janet Jackson's breast during the 2004 Super Bowl merely makes the point: there are no surprises other than the surprises intended.

A certain amount of direction is always necessary. Calls for a radically democratized, participatory spectacle notwithstanding, leaders are still needed. They don't have to provide lines and cues, but someone still must set the stage for participation. Spectacles are not spontaneous, they are planned (and the ones that are, like riots, are ugly). If spectacles are to be politically useful, they have to be directed toward a political goal. If they are to communicate a strong message, they need to be fashioned into a coherent brand. This presents a dilemma: how to organize an effective spectacle while still remaining open to the diversity of mass participation? The answer is the open spectacle.

Umberto Eco, the Italian academic critic (and author of the popular novel *The Name of the Rose*) makes a case for what he calls the *opera aperta*, or open work. While Eco is referring to works of art, it is a useful model for thinking through the idea of an ethical spectacle. All art, Eco argues, is open to interpretation. Yet in traditional forms of art this interpretation is tightly circumscribed. This doesn't mean that all art is literal; a medieval European writer, for instance, might use allegory in his text. But the meaning of the symbols employed by the artist are known to the reader, who can then decode the meaning of the text and arrive at the "proper" interpretation. The work of art is complete, and there is a right reading to be had. (Indeed, in the Middle Ages, "wrong" readings could be punished by charges of heresy and the application of the rack.)[12]

The open work, exemplified by so much of modern art, has no such finitude: it is left open by the artist to be completed by someone else. Eco uses examples of musical compositions that consist of groupings of notes that need to be put into sequence by the performer (Stockhausen's *Klavierstück XI*), books in which the reader must struggle to make sense of the author's elliptical universe (Joyce's *Ulysses* and *Finnegans Wake*), or sculptures whose forms are continually in movement and so must be constantly re-appreciated and reinterpreted (Calder's mobiles). These works are, by their very design, unfinished. Not just their meaning but the very form they take on is necessarily ambiguous. Whereas such multiplicity of popular interpretation was once seen as a problem that the artist (and the ecclesiastic or artistic establishment) had to overcome, this openness to meaning is now built into the art itself, which consists of "unplanned or physically incomplete structural units."[13] The noise of indeterminacy is part of the signal.

As such, open works, like Calder's mobiles, are always in movement. Their form and meaning is meant to change with the performer, the audience, and their surroundings. Convention is displaced by contingency.[14] This, however, does not mean chaos. No matter how open to the public, no matter how much form and meaning are in motion, there is still a generative text, and this text sets some guidelines. As Eco explains it:

> We can say that the "work in movement" is the possibility of numerous personal interventions, but it is not an amorphous invitation to indiscriminate participation. The invitation offers the performer the opportunity for an oriented assertion into something which always remains the world intended by the author.

Or, more succinctly if a bit more cryptically: "The *possibilities* which the work's openness make available work within a given *field of relations*."[15] The artist is still the creator, but what he creates is not so much a boundaried, static object, but a range of possibilities.

This is exactly how an open spectacle should work: planned, guided, and artfully created, but open to modification, indeterminacy, and contingency at both the level of form and meaning. A spectacle always in motion. One couldn't offer a better description of Critical Mass, a massive free-form bike ride in which cyclists, through the power of their numbers—their critical mass—take over city streets. Begun in San Francisco in 1992 under the awkward and thankfully short-lived name "Commute Clot," Critical Masses have happened or are regularly happening in 215 cities in North America, 143 in Europe, 22 in Asia, 20 in Australia, 8 in South America (mostly in Brazil), and 1 in Johannesburg, South Africa.[16] The "mass" can be as small as a handful of riders or as large as the three thousand that showed up at a New York City ride during the 2004 Republican National Convention.

Critical Mass rides are a way to bring attention to the second-class status of bicyclists on urban streets. When traffic flows in cities are planned, the car is king and, with a few exceptions, the needs of bicyclists are an afterthought, if thought of at all. The massive occupation of a street by bicyclists for a ride is a spectacular way to demonstrate their right to the road. As a flier passed out on San Francisco rides in the early nineties put it: "Critical Mass isn't BLOCKING traffic—We ARE traffic."[17] But these are not the only, or even the most important, politics of Critical Mass. It is the *experience* of participating that has the most profound effect.

I can remember riding through the neon canyons of Times Square on a Friday evening with Critical Mass in New York City, bicyclists to the front and back stretching for blocks. In the middle of that mass I felt part of a living organism. Making my way to the front of the mass I found that I was in control; along with the other bicyclists in the vanguard I helped decide where we should go when the police blocked our proposed route. Tiring of this, I slipped back, letting others make these decisions, content just to follow. The city was an integral part of the ride: depending on whether we were on the wide thoroughfare of Broadway or the narrow crosstown streets, our mass would bunch or stretch accordingly. Even the police, standing by peacefully, intervening forcefully, or fruitlessly trying to "lead" us with their flashing lights, were part of the event. That night with Critical Mass, I felt I was in a different city, an open city. As performance theorist and political activist L.M. Bogad notes, we were not merely occupying space, we were "opening space" to different experiences and meanings than those inscribed by authorities and made normal through custom.[18] For one October evening, my associations between the city and transportation, politics and fun, were profoundly altered. Streets were no longer a place of cars, laws, and getting to point B, but a space of bikes, fun, and discovery. We had politicized the environment.

Critical Mass is an open work. Despite loud disclaimers, it also has organizers. The environmental group Time's Up! does the bulk of the work in New York City, and, like the activists of Reclaim the Streets (a number of whom are one and the same), these organizers set the day and the time of the ride, the meeting place, and the general contours of the route to be followed. They follow up with legal help if the police arrest riders and explain the "meaning" of the event to reporters afterward. They give shape to what has been called an "organized coincidence."[19] But what Critical Mass looks like on any given night and the exact direction and duration the ride takes are indeterminate, contingent on who shows up (police included) and what the mass decides to do. The spectacle of Critical Mass is literally a "work in movement."

The indeterminacy of the form is mirrored by the ambiguity of the event's politics. This ideological openness has even been given a name by the Critical Mass "movement" (the term preferred to "organization" by its participants). In a play on both the number and the copying machine, they call it a "Xerocracy." The idea is explained in a 1994 pamphlet:

Organizational politics, with its official leaders, demands, etc., has been eschewed in favor of a more decentralized system. There is no one in charge. Ideas are spread, routes shared, and consensus sought through the ubiquitous copy machines on every job or at copy shops in every neighborhood—a "Xerocracy," in which anyone is free to make copies of their ideas and pass them around. Leaflets, flyers, stickers and zines all circulate madly both before, during and after the ride, rendering leaders unnecessary by ensuring that strategies and tactics are understood by as many people as possible.

Xerocracy promotes freedom and undercuts hierarchy because the mission is not set by a few in charge, but rather is broadly defined by its participants. The ride is not narrowly seen as an attempt to lobby for more bike lanes (although that goal exists) or to protest this or that aspect of the social order (although such sentiments are often expressed). Rather, each person is free to invent his or her own reasons for participating and is also free to share those ideas with others.[20]

Amazingly, it all somehow works. Rides happen, messages are circulated, riders find power and solidarity in a mass, spectators see a street deeded over to bike traffic, and for an evening the city opens up just a little bit.

Critical Mass, as widespread as it is, is still a marginal movement. But the openness it exemplifies taps into the much wider desire for exploration, autonomy, and modification that we saw expressed in contemporary video games. But an open spectacle like Critical Mass takes things a step further, for, in the end, the video game player is only as free as the algorithms of the programmer allow him to be, the ideal of transformative play notwithstanding. An open spectacle is different. An organizer sets the "field of relations" and accounts for possibilities, but these are not set in computer code, and the best-laid plans, even the most open of plans, can be—must be—opened even further. While this is what gives the open spectacle its egalitarian character and fuels its dynamism, it also raises a host of potential problems.

With the spectacle open to whoever shows up, the spectacle is also open to attitudes and behaviors at odds with most of the participants. Critical Mass, for example, draws from a pretty diverse population of bike riders: working-class bike messengers, executives on their fancy mountain bikes, high school students on tricked-out BMXs, and bohemian welder/sculptors on their custom hodgepodge contraptions. It also draws a small number of very angry bicyclists (or agents provocateurs, as the more suspicious-minded members of Critical Mass believe) who seem to enjoy aggravating motorists by pounding on cars and yelling at drivers.[21]

Open spectacles are also open to a multiplicity of meanings. This, in part, is a reflection of the diversity of the participants, each with his or her own variant of message—the "Xerocracy" of Critical Mass. The globalization movement, for instance, has been frequently criticized for not having a unified message and thus not offering any coherent meaning. But this is an issue for any spectacle. For meaning is not only decided upon by organizers and participants, but also bestowed by the outside world. One Reclaim the Streets action staged in Times Square in solidarity with the anti-WTO protests in Seattle was mistaken by visiting tourists for an MTV shoot. With a tightly scripted spectacle, staying "on message" is hard enough; with a spectacle committed to openness, it is sometimes unclear that there is a message at all.[22]

All this openness seems like a recipe for meaningless disorder, but it needn't be. Order happens and meanings are imparted, just in a different manner than the closed spectacles of fascism and commercialism. It is instructive to witness what happens when an angry cyclist acts up on a Critical Mass ride. When this occurs, a group of riders usually forms around him, some to merely observe the commotion, but others—a critical mass—to smooth feathers and tell the errant biker to move on. Similarly, while there's always some nut job handing out flyers likening Critical Mass to the glorious people's revolution of North Korea, many more flyers make salient points about the ecological ramifications of automobiles and the benefits of nonviolent collective action. As a Critical Mass pedals by, some bystanders no doubt see the collapse of order into chaos, but many others, I'd argue, see an exuberant reclamation of public space. There will always be a range of actions and opinions and meanings and directions that occur in an open spectacle, and there will be freaky outliers on each side of this range, but the critical mass in the center gives coherence. The result is a bell curve of meaning.[23] Drawing from complexity theory in physics, one could liken it to a sort of emergent politics, one in which through a multitude of individual activities arises a community response.

A certain order and meaning arise through collective action, but to embrace the open spectacle means making peace with indeterminacy. Valuing diversity demands such acceptance. Homogeneity makes for a "smoother" spectacle: one can count on certain actions being understood and meanings shared. It is an easy brand to package and sell. Ethical spectacles demand something different: a commitment to plurality and contingency, and thus a bit of necessary messiness. This may work in its favor for it actualizes, better than any corporate brand, the ideal of Kevin Roberts's "lovemark" trinity of mystery, sensuality, and intimacy.

But unlike the product of a Saatchi & Saatchi advertising team, the open spectacle doesn't hope to *resemble* these things; it is, instead, the very expression of them.

Nazi spectacles, the historian George Mosse argues, always culminated in order. The masses might march here and line up there, but they always arrived at the same answer: the Nazi Party.[24] Ethical spectacle, as an *opera aperta*, never arrives at one answer. Open to the noisy diversity of participants, observers, and settings to create the completed work, it ends (or rather, rests) in a field of possibilities.

Transparent Spectacle

Benno von Arendt, the official stage designer for the Third Reich, saw his job as producing grand illusions for an audience, a canvas and wood manifestation of their dearest fantasies. This was an ideal carried out of Nazi theater (which never caught on with the masses) and into their far more successful festivals, pageants, rallies, and films. One can see this in Riefenstahl's *Triumph of the Will*, in which Nazi rallies are staged as an image of popular order and adulation for the leader: a negation of the disorder and weakness of leadership that marked Germany between the wars (a disorder helped along by the thuggery of the Nazi brownshirts). "The magic of theater must compensate for the reality of life," Mosse writes of Nazi spectacle.[25] Yet it is exactly an idealized and aestheticized reality that is presented in Nazi spectacle.

The power of *Triumph of the Will* is its appearance *as* reality. The film opens with scenes of a real German city, a real airplane brings the Führer down from the clouds, real crowds greet him with adulation, real stormtroopers stand at attention, real men frolic in the sun and eat sausages, and real functionaries of the party give speeches. "Not a single scene is staged," Riefenstahl claimed in an interview in a film magazine thirty years after directing *Triumph*. "Everything is genuine.... It is history—pure history."[26] This is revisionist nonsense. It was, of course, staged history, with the public given their cues—staged twice over, in fact, as from the beginning the rally was conceived (with Riefenstahl's help) as a giant film set. As Susan Sontag perceptively points out, the film is "not only the record of reality but is one reason for which reality has been constructed, and must eventually supercede it."[27] In this light Riefenstahl's claims are instructive: the Nazis presented, even to themselves, their spectacles as reality.

Creators of commercial spectacles are a bit more honest—at least with themselves. A few years back an interesting video appeared called *Production Notes*. By reading production notes pilfered from an advertising agency over visual footage of the ads to which they refer, the filmmaker, Jason Simon, provides a revealing look into the conceptualization of commercials. One set of directions for a Mars chocolate bar advertisement is particularly instructive. Shots of chocolate, caramel, and nuts are intercut with images of people enjoying "the best things in life"—walks on the beach, reading Sunday comics, and, of course, shopping. The narrator reads the production notes in a deadpan voice:

Campaign Look: We are aiming for something that might be called beautiful reality. On the one hand we want these moments that are life's best to look convincingly real, unstaged, spontaneous. The viewer should almost get the feeling that these are found moments of film, things that really happened when, as luck would have it, there just happened to be a camera rolling to film it. On the other hand we want the images to be rich, deeply textured and beautiful.[28]

"Beautiful reality" typifies the relationship commercial culture has to the real. As I've argued previously, the world of advertising is utopian. It is an image of what will happen to the consumer once he or she purchases the product: the magical transformation. Yet, for all this magic, a sense of the real is essential.[29] The consumers have to buy into the fantasy world being represented, not as a distant dream but as a future and possible reality for themselves. Because of this, advertisers take pains to cast actors who look like the audience, albeit a more perfect version ("In general the people should look real in an attractive sort of way," read the production notes), and set their ads in believable—if also desirable—locales: the Southwestern desert, a New York City street, a Southern California beach.[30] The fantasy of the advertiser's fantasy is that it isn't one.

But spectacle needn't pass itself off as reality to be effective in engaging the spectator. At least this was the hope of the playwright Bertolt Brecht. Brecht was disturbed by what he saw of the theater that surrounded him in Germany between the wars. With most theater (and movies and TV) the goal is to construct an illusion so complete that the audience will be drawn away from their world and into the fantasy on stage. This seduction is essential to traditional dramaturgy. First theorized by Aristotle in his *Poetics*, it stresses audience identification with the drama on stage: when an actor cries, you are supposed to cry; when he triumphs, you triumph as well. This allure is aided by staging that strives toward realism or captivates the audience with lavish displays of full-blown fantasy (*Reichsdramaturg* von Arendt, like Hitler, was a devotee of the phantasmagoric operas of Richard Wagner). Such drama "works" insofar as the audience is well entertained, but there is a political cost. Entranced, the audience suspends critical thought, and all action is sequestered to the stage. A "cowed, credulous, hypnotized mass," Brecht described these spectators, "these people seem relieved of activity and like men to whom something is being done."[31] It's a pretty accurate description of the problem with most spectacle.

As a progressive, Brecht was horrified by this response of the theatergoing audience. He wanted to use his plays to motivate people to change the world, not escape from it. He understood that no matter how radical the content of his plays might be, if his audience lost itself in the illusion of his play and allowed the actors to do the action for them, then they would leave their politics up on the stage when the play was over. Brecht was hardly the first critic to comment upon this. One of the many faults of the theater, the great Enlightenment philosopher Jean-Jacques Rousseau wrote in 1758, is that it permits its audience to experience public virtue vicariously while ignoring it in their day-to-day lives, allowing them to cry copiously over misfortune on the stage and then steel their hearts once outside. "In giving our tears to these fictions," he writes, "we have satisfied all the rights of humanity without having to give anything more of ourselves." Since a democracy depends upon its citizens' engagement in civic society, Rousseau believed that drama was dangerous to a republic.[32]

Rousseau saw the political problems of the popular theater as intractable; Brecht did not. Brecht believed that one could change the way drama is done and thus change its impact on the audience. Borrowing from the Chinese stage, he developed a dramaturgical method called epic theater.[33] Central to epic theater was *Verfremdungseffekt*, a term he mercifully shortened to the V-effect, which, translated into English, means roughly "alienation effect." Instead of drawing people into a seamless illusion, Brecht strove to push them away—to alienate them—so that they would never forget that they were watching a play.

To accomplish the V-effect, Brecht and others, notably the Berlin director Erwin Piscator, who staged many of Brecht's plays, developed a whole battery of innovative techniques: giving away the ending of the play at the beginning, having actors remind the audience that they are actors, humorous songs which interrupt tragic scenes, music which runs counter to mood, cue cards informing the audience that a scene is changing, stagehands appearing on stage to move props, and so on. Brecht even championed the idea of a "smokers' theater" with the stage shrouded in thick smoke exhaled by a cigar-puffing audience—anything to break the seamless illusion of traditional theater.[34]

While the function of the V-effect was to alienate his audience, it is a misreading of Brecht's intentions to think that he wanted to create a theater that couldn't be enjoyed. Nothing could be further from his mind. He heaped ridicule on an avant garde who equated unpopularity with artistic integrity and insisted that the job of the dramaturge is to entertain, demanding that theater be "enjoyable to the senses."[35] For both political and dramaturgical reasons he rejected the preaching model of persuasion; he wanted his audiences to have fun, not attend a lecture. Deconstructing the mind/body binary, Brecht believed that one could speak to reason *and* the senses. One could see through the spectacle and enjoy it nonetheless: a transparent spectacle.

A nice idea in theory, but does it work? I think so. A well-directed Brecht play is a great deal of fun, a different sort of fun than watching an Andrew Lloyd Weber suck-you-in spectacle, more Aha! and less Oooh!, but fun nonetheless. But let's forget theater, a rarified art form which few people enjoy anyway. A better example of the potential popularity of a transparent spectacle is professional wrestling. Professional wrestling is big business in the United States, with World Wrestling Entertainment, Inc. (formerly the World Wrestling Foundation), bringing in an estimated $340 million in revenue in 2000, and reaching ten million viewers each week on TV, making professional wrestling, according to *American Demographics*, the most popular programming on cable.[36] Wrestling mania isn't limited to the United States: pro wrestling has long been popular entertainment in Mexico and parts of Latin America, and the WWE is expanding its reach overseas to Europe. Pro wrestlers have gone on to be celebrities (Hulk Hogan), movie stars (The Rock), governors (Jesse Ventura), and, in Mexico, critics of the ruling party (the original Superbarrio Man). And it's all fake: the characters, the rivalries, the matches are phony. Everybody (over the age of twelve) knows this, yet it doesn't stop fans from rooting for their favorites, hissing at the villains, and buying tickets to matches. In other words, knowing that it's a spectacle doesn't get in the way of the fans having a lot of fun. Like the architainment of Las Vegas, the enduring popularity of professional wrestling suggests that illusion is not the same thing as delusion.

Brecht's V-effect has been adopted, in some cases quite consciously, by some of the more theatrical activist groups.[37] Recall the Billionaires for Bush. Wearing long gowns and tiaras, tuxedos and top hats, the activists playing billionaires don't hope to pass themselves off as the real thing. Real billionaires wear artfully distressed designer jeans; these Billionaires look like characters out of a game of *Monopoly*. Because their artifice is obvious, there is no deception of their audience. They are not seen as people who *are*, but instead as people who *are presenting*. Because of this the Billionaires' message of wealth inequality and the corruption of money on politics is not passively absorbed by spectators identifying with character or scene, but consciously understood by an audience watching an obvious performance.

Furthermore, the spectacle the Billionaires present is so patently playacted, so unnatural, that the absurd unnaturality of a caucus of "people of wealth" advocating for their own rights is highlighted. This is, of course, what American democracy has become: a system where money buys power to protect money. This is no secret, but that's part of the problem. The corruption of democracy is so well known that it is tacitly accepted as the natural course of things. One of the functions of the V-effect is to alienate the familiar: to take what is common sense and ask why it is so common—as Brecht put it: "to free socially conditioned phenomena from that stamp of familiarity which protects them against our grasp today."[38] By acting out the roles of obviously phony billionaires buying politicians for their own advantage, the Billionaires encourage the viewer of their spectacle to step back and look critically at the taken-for-grantedness of a political system where money has a voice, prodding them to question: "Isn't it really the current political system that's absurd?" The transparency of the spectacle allows the spectator to look through what is being presented to the reality of what is there.[39]

The spectacular claims of the Billionaires are backed up with fact sheets detailing the correlation between campaign contributions and political favors. However, even sober facts are presented in faux-character. "Legislation: A Lucrative Investment" one such pamphlet reads, explaining: "If a mutual fund returns 20% a year, that's considered unbelievably good. But in the low-risk, high return world of legislation, a 20% return is positively lousy." The return on legislation is laid out in the form of an investment portfolio report. For example, Bechtel Corporation made a $3,310,102 "investment" in campaign contributions between 1990 and 2002. But in 2002 and 2003 they received a "return" of $1,029,833,000 in contracts for infrastructure construction in Iraq—a whopping 31,012 percent return. "If you can get this kind of a return when you buy a few congressmen, just imagine what you get when you buy the president. Don't wait. Invest now, and let the paybacks roll in for the next four years," urge the Billionaires.[40]

By wrapping their facts in shtick (while also footnoting them) the Billionaires speak to our dual desires to be entertained *and* to know. They even appeal to our penchant for wanting to know what's behind the scenes—not with a breathless exposé of celebrity scandal, nor with an authoritative investigation like those in the *Times*, but by letting the spectator in on the joke: these Billionaires aren't really billionaires; they are progressive activists, and they're here to make a point. The stock Billionaires for Bush flyer begins by rhetorically asking the question: "Who are we?" It concludes by answering: "Who are we really?"[41] The line they walk between reality and illusion is shaky. Neither a revelation of the real nor traditional theater of illusion, the spectacle of the Billionaires is both, and neither. It resonates someplace in between.

The Irish Hunger Memorial, jutting up from the lower tip of Manhattan, provides another example of how a transparent spectacle might work. Designed by Brian Tolle and opened in 2002, the memorial commemorates the million-plus Irish who died during the potato blight of the 1840s, victims of mono-crop agriculture and the free-market response of the British colonizing authority. The memorial is composed of two parts. The bottom is a dark fieldstone base, cut through with horizontal bands of fluorescent light shining through frosted glass. More than a hundred quotations—songs, poems, statistics, parliamentary reports, autobiographical tales of suffering—are backlit on the glass. The visitor enters an inclined tunnel where the words of the past are joined by audio voices speaking of famine and hunger today. The end of the tunnel leads into a partially completed (or dismantled) fieldstone crofter's cottage. A path winds out of the cottage and back up a slanting quarter-acre plot that recalls the landscape of rural Ireland, ending at a vista overlooking the mouth of the Hudson River and, in the distance, Ellis Island.

As a piece of art and a statement of politics the memorial is a mixed bag. The neon-segmented polished stone base brings to mind an ultra-chic Ian Schrager hotel lobby. The text—two miles of it laid out in a line—is overwhelming, and the tunnel, where the text is accompanied by audio, feels like some sort of Gutenberg-era funhouse. The result is overload, a blur of bad things, ironically resulting in a sort of blasé acceptance of the inevitability of hunger. But the top of the monument is something different entirely: a serene and empty landscape where you can almost feel the presence of the dead. With its ruined cottage and bleached stones scattered about, it recalls a graveyard. Hunger stops being an abstraction and is revealed for what it is: a cause of mass death.

The flora atop the Hunger Memorial is native to Ireland, each of the bleached stones is from one of her counties, and the cottage is an authentic famine-era structure shipped piece by piece from County Mayo. Predictably, this has led critics to comment on the imitative quality of Tolle's monument. A "meld of simulacrum and real," David Frankel called it in *ArtForum*.[42] But what's interesting about the memorial is that it is neither real nor simulacrum. It works when and where it does precisely because it makes no such claims on the real; the Hunger Memorial is clearly symbolic. The landscape is framed by skyscrapers, each stone has the name of the county it came from chiseled clearly into its face, and the cottage is purposefully undone. The result is that you can never slip into a fantasy that you are in 1840s Ireland. You *can't* fool yourself into feeling what it must have felt like to feel hunger and desperation.

Without simulation and its attendant appeals to representing the real, there is no manipulation. Nor is there the complementary opposite: cynical withdrawal following the recognition that you are being manipulated (what I call the Spielberg effect). Yet, unlike the miles of neon-lit text below, Tolle's ghostly meadow has an effect that pulls deeper than fact. The plants, the cottage, the stones speak *of* a real time and a real history, but they make no claims to speak *for* it. What Brecht wrote of epic theater could apply equally well to Tolle's monument: "It emphasizes the general gist of showing, which always underlies that which is being shown."[43] By symbolizing the landscape depopulated by death instead of simulating it, the Irish Hunger Memorial opened a space and lends visitors the props with which to *consider* hunger and the politics of famine.

Not all progressive spectacles need be so theoretically informed or semiotically complex as the Billionaires for Bush or the Irish Hunger Memorial; these are just two examples of how a spectacle might work in a way that is both emotionally stirring and ethically honest. It is enough to acknowledge that the fantasy being presented is a fantasy: a performance, not reality; a symbol, not simulation. Unlike the opaque spectacles of commercialism and fascism, which always make claims to the truth, a progressive spectacle invites the viewer to see through it: to acknowledge its essential "falsity" while being moved by it nonetheless. Most spectacle strives for seamlessness; ethical spectacle reveals its own workings. Most spectacle employs illusion in the pretense of portraying reality; ethical spectacle demonstrates the reality of its own illusions. Ethical spectacle reminds the viewer that the spectacle is never reality, but always a spectacle. In this way, ironically, spectacle becomes real.

Real Spectacle

Why was the spectacle of a dead soldier's mother camping out-side President Bush's vacation ranch in the summer of 2005 so effective in garnering favorable media attention, capturing public sympathy, and turning public opinion against the war in Iraq? It is hard to pin it down to one reason. Part of it was timing: that sum-mer gas prices were rising, the weekly body counts in Iraq were getting worse, and the public was tiring of the administration's rosy assurances on the war. Some of it was media access: the world's media was camped out in rural Texas to cover a president on vacation who wouldn't give them a good story, so they turned their attention and cameras to someone who would. The specta-cle's success gained from a public relations failure: the refusal of the president to meet with a dead soldier's grieving mother was a serious bungle by the normally spectacle-adept White House. And the story of grief for a loved one lost in war is a classic narrative, dramatized since Sophocles's *Antigone* (even, with a twist, by Ber-tolt Brecht in *Mother Courage*). But these were merely contributing factors to the perfect storm. At the center of the story was some-thing far more profound and far more important: Cindy Sheehan herself, a mother who lost her twenty-four-year-old son in a war waged by a man who refused to meet her. In other words, at the core of the spectacle was something real.

Not that conservative pundits didn't do their best to deny this. Rush Limbaugh went on record stating that Cindy Sheehan's "story is nothing more than forged documents—there's nothing about it that's real." The conservative cartoonists Cox and Forkum sketched a picture of Sheehan with her dead son across her lap and Michael Moore in the background directing her: "This time . . . let's see some *tears*." Yet this time the smears didn't stick; "The Swift Boating of Cindy Sheehan," as *Times* columnist Frank Rich put it, didn't work.[44] Public support stayed behind Ms. Sheehan and the president's approval ratings on his handling of the war kept dropping.

The conservatives did have a point. Like Rosa Parks before her, Sheehan was no ingenue. Even before her son was killed she was against the war, and she had a history of organizational and leadership experience. She had been a Catholic youth leader for eight years and, after her son's death, formed the Gold Star Families for Peace, an antiwar organization for families who lost loved ones in the war.[45] Media coverage of her vigil was not exactly left to chance, either. Fenton Communications, a progressive public relations firm, was hired by the antiwar group TrueMajority to help coordinate media coverage of Sheehan's activism.[46] But at the bottom of it all, beneath the chance of circumstance and the strategic communications, and cutting through the smears and spins, was an undeniable, unalterable, reality: Army Spc. Casey Austin Sheehan was dead.

By reality, I mean simply two things. First, that something is what it claims to be. Therefore, as I argued earlier, a phantasmagoric spectacle that proclaims itself to be a phantasmagoric spectacle is real, whereas a spectacle that claims to be reality is not. And, second, by reality I mean that something exists. Whether material (a dead soldier) or immaterial (public opinion about the meaning of that dead soldier), reality is something that can be verified, tested, and otherwise empirically argued to exist.

Most spectacle, both political and commercial, has a slippery relationship to reality. Spectacle is often created to pass itself off as reality, mobilized to mask an inconvenient alternative reality or the fact that there is no reality at all.[47] Recall the top-gun landing of George W. Bush on the USS *Abraham Lincoln*. The fantasy of a war hero arriving by fighter plane to announce the end of a successful war was an attempt to create a reality to stand in for its lack: Bush is not a war hero, and the mission in Iraq—as Cindy Sheehan can attest—was certainly not accomplished.

Ethical spectacle works differently. It does not pass itself off as reality. Sheehan's roadside protest, bristling with antiwar signs and crosses symbolizing those killed in action in Iraq, was clearly a political protest, not the accidental resting place of a grieving mother. And in her speeches, Sheehan is at pains to point out that while it is grief and anger that got her where she is now, she is speaking as an antiwar activist engaged in a political act (something, ironically, which her critics point to as further evidence of her inauthenticity). Sheehan's protest against the war that killed her son makes no claims to being unconstructed. This is why revelations of her activist past or her use of PR firms to publicize her opinions had no lasting damage. Cindy Sheehan's vigil was a protest and thus, as a protest, it is real. It cannot be "exposed"—it is already what it appears to be.

Yet the demand for reality behind spectacle goes deeper than this. For spectacle to be ethical it must not only reveal itself as what it is but also have as its foundation something real. At this point it is worth reiterating my initial argument that to embrace spectacle does not mean a radical rejection of the empirical real and the verifiably true. It is merely acknowledging that the real and the true are not self-evident: they need to be told and sold. The goal of the ethical spectacle is not to replace the real with the spectacle, but to reveal and amplify the real *through* the spectacle. Think of this as an inversion of Secretary of State Colin Powell's infamous case to the United Nations for war in Iraq. Armed with reasoned reports and documentary photos of Saddam Hussein's nuclear ambitions, Powell employed the tools of fact to make the case for the full-blown fantasy of Iraq's possession of weapons of mass destruction. Ethical spectacle employs the opposite strategy: the tools of spectacle as a way to mobilize support for the facts. As such, an ethical spectacle must start with reality.

In Sheehan's case this is a straightforward process: her son was killed, she is distraught and angry, and the president who sent her son into battle won't meet with her. All reality needed here was amplification, and the scene of Sheehan's protest at the foot of Bush's driveway did exactly that. In Christian parlance, her mere presence *bore witness* to the cost of war. But other realities are not as easy to illuminate and must be showcased. This is what Martin Luther King Jr. and his young Southern Christian Leadership Conference (SCLC) lieutenants did in Birmingham, Alabama, in 1963. Well aware of Commissioner of Public Safety "Bull" Conner's reputation for virulent bigotry and a violent temper, the SCLC staged a series of peaceful demonstrations aimed at desegregating the public facilities of the city. Predictably, Bull Conner and his troops responded with fire hoses and attack dogs. Through what social movement scholar Doug McAdam calls "a genius for strategic dramaturgy," King and the SCLC were able to demonstrate visually to a global media the violent reality of American racism hidden from and often overlooked by much of the world.[48]

Even more abstract forces and hidden processes, such as the influence of money in politics or the slow degradation of the environment, call for even more intervention; spectacle must be staged in order to dramatize the unseen and expose associations elusive to the eye. "When public affairs are popularized," Walter Lippmann once explained, "their transformation into a human interest requires first abstraction from the original, and then animation of what has been abstracted."[49] Billionaires for Bush, for instance, use their theatrical clowning to animate the abstraction of money ruling our democracy—making visible an invisible reality. Even the carnivalesque demonstrations of Reclaim the Streets and Critical Mass, the sociable train parties and the massive globalization protests, seek to draw people's attention toward the reality of the privatization of space, auto-centric transportation policies, alienating environments, or nonrepresentative trade organizations. They do this not only by staging protests with explicit messages, but by creating absurd spectacles that implicitly ask people to reflect back upon the "normal" reality of space for business, streets for cars, subways for zoning out, and politics for experts. This is spectacle as estrangement—creating an unreality that exposes the bizarre reality of everyday existence.

There is also a simpler, and purely pragmatic, reason for the edifice of spectacle to be built upon a foundation of truth. It lasts longer. By the time of the Republican National Convention, only one year after the commander-in-chief's orchestrated landing on the USS *Abraham Lincoln*, the images were unusable. In the interim, details of the staging of the photo-op had leaked out, Bush's tawdry military record had been made public, and the war in Iraq had escalated. Truth may not out, but lies built upon nothing have a tendency to come undone. Even Nazi propaganda chief Joseph Goebbels, who once argued that if you repeat a lie often enough it becomes true, discovered this to his dismay. After the disastrous defeat of the German army at Stalingrad became known, no amount of propaganda Goebbels produced did much good in convincing the German people that their side was still winning the war.[50] As the namesake of the aircraft carrier where Bush staged his heroism once put it: you can't fool all of the people all of the time.

Ethical spectacle must not only root itself in the real but also lead back to it. One of the dangers of a politics of spectacle is that one can be seduced into believing that all politics are cultural: an ethereal game of clashing ideologies and cognitive frames, meaning systems and manifested fantasies. This can lead to what the activist and author Leslie Kauffman calls "ether activism," an activism so consumed with struggling over hearts and minds that it forgets there is another struggle to win: concrete political power and thus the ability to effect material change. It is certainly true that politics must be given meaning if they are to be either sustained or changed—especially within a democracy where public opinion can be power. But political meaning is empty, *unrealized*, unless expressed in policies and politics with material results. We need to think of our spectacles as not only reckoning back to a material real, but moving forward as part of an overall plan to change not just the way people think, but also the way they act to ultimately transform the shape of material reality itself.

The link between spectacle and "real" results can be a tight one. Cindy Sheehan's vigil attempted to change public opinion about the war in Iraq to pressure elected politicians to bring the troops home so no more sons and daughters have to die. These associations can also be a bit looser. Critical Mass wants to alter perceptions of what a street is for and posit a vision of what a more socially and ecologically just society might look like. Sometimes it's a stretch, but if ethical spectacle is to have any connection to progressive politics and policy, and not exist as some sort of activist version of a vicarious video game, then we must always ask the question: if this spectacle is successful, then what is really going to change?

And finally, it is worth repeating that an ethical spectacle must address the *real* dreams and desires of people—not the dreams and desires that progressives think they should, could, or "if they knew what was good for them" would have, but the ones people actually do have, no matter how trivial, politically incorrect, or even impossible they seem. How we address these dreams and desires is a political decision, but we must acknowledge and respond to them if we want people to identify with our politics. To engage the real as part of ethical spectacle is not the same thing as being limited by the current confines of reality. For reality is not the end but a point of beginning—a firm foundation on which to build the possible, or to stand upon while dreaming the impossible.

Dream Spectacle

I have a dream that one day this nation will rise up and live out the true meaning of its creed: "We hold these truths to be self-evident: that all men are created equal." I have a dream that one day on the red hills of Georgia the sons of former slaves and the sons of former slave owners will be able to sit down together at a table of brotherhood. I have a dream that one day even the state of Mississippi, a desert state, sweltering with the heat of injustice and oppression, will be transformed into an oasis of freedom and justice. I have a dream that my four children will one day live in a nation where they will not be judged by the color of their skin but by the content of their character. I have a dream today.[51]

These words need little introduction. They are taught in grade schools, replayed on television specials, and even appear in advertisements; they are an integral part of America's self-understanding. As such, the idea of political dreaming has become enshrined in American culture. But Martin Luther King Jr.'s dream was hardly America's first. It was, after all, finding and founding a divine "City on the Hill" that motivated the Puritan immigrants of New England. Dreams of a baser sort inspired Spanish conquistadors and Southern planters, but these fantasies of riches were dreams nonetheless. King understood the powerful history of American dreaming when he gave his speech in Washington, D.C., on that August day in 1963. He quoted verse and borrowed his prophetic style from the Bible, yet he also referenced the secular imaginings animating his country, drawing upon the Declaration of Independence and the Constitution again and again.[52] His dream, he underscored, "is a dream deeply rooted in the American dream." Few countries put such faith in dreams as ours.

Progressives today seem to have forgotten how to dream. One need look no further than the sorry state of the Democratic Party for evidence of this absence. Since the seventies the party has been bereft of imagination, vacillating between tepid calls for the retention of a watered-down welfare state and strategic co-optations of Republican policies. These aren't dreams, they're reactions. Progressives further to the left offer little better. "Another World Is Possible"—that was the slogan adopted by the globalization movement. It was a conscious creation, the result of widespread discussions within the movement about how to counter the press portrayal of us as an *antimovement*. But as soon as the new, more "positive" slogan was trundled out, fault lines started to show. Exactly *what* possible world were we imagining? What would it look like? How would we get there? The movement that had staged such impressive demonstrations on the ground had little imagination up in the air. If progressives want to be a political force again we need to rediscover how to dream. But saying this and doing it are two different things, and the latter is far more difficult, for there are real reasons why progressive dreams have dried up.

Martin Luther King Jr.'s dream hit all the right notes. It was personalized, it made associations between civil rights for African Americans and wider American ideals, it promised a (nonmagical) transformation into the promised land. It did a masterful job of "branding" the civil rights struggle. But what gave King's speech such immense power was that his dream was realistic. He was merely demanding that black Americans be able to enjoy what white Americans ostensibly already had: a chance. As an experienced organizer and astute student of social movements (and prophetic rhetoric), King understood that to cast his dream as something eminently possible was to give it a chance of becoming a reality. This is the strength of his dream. It is also its weakness.

The problem with realistic dreams is that they are always in danger of *the claim* of being realized. With Colin Powell and Condoleezza Rice at the helm of the U.S. State Department, Clarence Thomas sitting on the Supreme Court, and Oprah Winfrey in charge of her own highly profitable entertainment company, one might make the argument that we now "live in a nation where [African Americans] will not be judged by the color of their skin but by the content of their character." The stamps, the streets, the parks, and the national holiday named after Martin Luther King Jr. are only possible because his dream is no longer the challenge to the status quo that it was in 1963. Pointing out the rainbow faces of the new elite, one can make a legitimate (though not necessarily accurate) claim that the dream has been realized. Thus for some, King's dream is complete, while for others who experience or witness the enduring poverty, undereducation, and unemployment of black Americans, it was always a sham. Either way, the dream is over. As the satirical newspaper *The Onion* declared on the occasion of Rosa Parks's death, as her body lay in wait in the Capitol Rotunda and President Bush placed a wreath upon her casket, "Now We Can Finally Put Civil Rights Behind Us."[53]

King may have kept his dream confined within the realm of the possible for tactical and rhetorical reasons, but there's another compelling reason to do so. It is extremely difficult to dream about what you do not, in some way, know. You can dream of pink elephants without ever having met one, but only because you know the animal and the color and can combine the two. There is a long philosophical history to this conundrum, stretching from René Descartes's meditations on perception and deception through Karl Marx's antiutopianism to Michel Foucault's microphysics of power, but the basic premise is fairly simple: our imagination is necessarily constricted by our current situation. Dreams of social change, insofar as they are reasonable, rational, and cogent, are always those of a change within the terms of the very society that one is trying to change. Thus they don't envision much of a change at all.

The politicotheoretical response to this problem of "totality," as it has been called, is varied. Marx accepted this condition as a given. One always sees the future from the present, and therefore the task at hand is to understand the present: its fissures, contradictions, and potentialities. This is why the so-called father of communism devoted thousands of pages to the analysis of capitalism and only a handful to imagining communism. It is within and through capitalism that the proletariat develops a different consciousness, and it is through their struggle against capitalism that the proletariat begins to create communism. One can only know the future when one has built it.

Radical thinkers who followed Marx, disenchanted with the seeming lack of desire on the part of the proletariat to build the socialist future and their apparently active desire to embrace the consumer goodies that capitalism offered, looked to those "outside" the system for vision. This school of thought found its apogee in the 1960s when Third World peasants, racial minorities, artists, students, even the insane and criminal were championed as agents of revolution. Kept on the margins of the totalizing system, these people (so it was believed) were in a unique position to dream and fight for a different world.

Today, however, the Other seems to have failed its historical mission, either creating "revolutionary" authoritarian societies or embracing capitalism when let in from the margins—or both, as in the surreal case of China, where the frenzied embrace of capitalism is directed by the Communist Party. In what might be described as a continuing slide toward total disillusionment, politically minded intellectuals in more recent times have lowered their sights, abandoning the dreams of revolution and championing mere *resistance* as an end in itself. This resistance, which can be located in subcultural styles of dress and music, the antisocial gangbanging glorified in *Grand Theft Auto*, or mere general political apathy, is seen as part of "the Great Refusal" on the part of citizens to do what they are told.[54] The provocative postmodernist Jean Baudrillard has gone as far as to suggest that the refusal to be an active political subject (discussing, voting, building) is best understood as an unconscious political strategy aimed at a society which demands active subjects yet denies them any real power. Devolution, argues Baudrillard, has replaced revolution.[55]

Although I am hesitant to embrace Baudrillard's playful cynicism, I'm hard-pressed to refute his basic assertion that most forms of progressive politics these days take the form of negation. In their recent book *Empire*, Michael Hardt and Antonio Negri argue that the present system of capitalism constitutes a new sort of diffused and omnipresent empire. There is no way to be outside this empire, and thus rebellion within this system often takes the form of a generalized "being-against."[56] The difficulties of the globalization movement to move past its anti–Free Trade stance and the Democratic Party to situate itself as anything other than not-Republican (or in its worst moments as Republicans-lite), seems to suggest that a positive progressive politics of *being for* is an unrealizable dream.

Yet there is a type of dreaming happening on the outskirts of progressive politics. These dreams don't look like those of King, nor do they resemble the resistant nightmares of pure negation, but in these odd dreams may be a model for a different way to imagine and inspire.

It is a cold night outside, but inside St. Mark's Church in New York City, it is stifling. An overflow crowd has come to hear Reverend Billy preach. Punctuated by emphatic "amens" from the crowd, the good reverend energetically exhorts his flock to resist temptation. His choir, dressed in bright yellow and purple robes, launches into a spirited hymn and the audience joins in. Not an unusual scene for a church, except for a few things: Reverend Billy is a performance artist named Bill Talen, behind the pulpit is a ten-foot-high crucifix with a large stuffed Mickey Mouse nailed squarely upon it, and the sermon is on the evils of shopping. With the cadences, mannerisms, and impressive pompadour of a tel-evangelist, the reverend launches into his sermon:

> There is only one sin, children! Shopping. All sins are a form of shop-ping! The utopian jolt at the point of purchase when the product smiles at us—we are actually walking that moment into the Lake of Fire. Don't you feel the fire? Don't you feel the pain? . . .
>
> This is Manhattan as Suburban Mall. This is a fatal disease known as Involuntary Entertainment. This is the disease known as Continuous Shopping. This is drowning in the Sea of Identical Details.
>
> This is the moment. We stop shopping. The revolution of no shopping. We can start trying to remember what we imagined. We can begin to recall what desire was when it was not supervised.[57]

At first read, this is just another arch-ironic send-up of organized religion staged in front of a crowd of urban hipsters. And it is. "We use right-wing hate preachers' images and turn them inside out," Bill explains.[58] But it is also something much more: the service is a genuine experience of communion and shared faith around a vision of a world not centered on consumption. Everyone knows that Bill is not a real reverend and they are not real churchgoers, yet it doesn't seem to matter. It is still deeply moving. Talen has created, in his own words, a "god that people who do not believe in god believe in."[59]

Reverend Billy has created this communion by demanding con-sumer abstinence. This is an absurd demand. He isn't asking for restrained shopping or thoughtful shopping but "the revolution of no shopping." His congregation is not some ancient agrarian pop-ulation where such self-sufficiency is a possibility; Bill's sermon is directed to an urban American audience for whom buying stuff is a necessity. In other ways Reverend Billy has his political feet on the ground. He champions the efforts of local merchants to keep their stores open, joins campaigns to keep Wal-Mart out of communities, works closely with activist groups to expose Disney's offshore production of their products, and pressures Starbucks to use worker- and environment-friendly Fair Trade coffee. But at the core of his politics is an impossible dream: stop shopping.

The reverend's sermons resonate with the reasoning behind the recent crop of advertisements that "promise" the ridiculous. If no one believes the appeals of preachers, politicians, and advertisers anyway, then you might as well push it over the top and get a chuckle. And part of this is pure provocation, a bit of absurd theatricality to draw our attention to how much we shop and how often we think about shopping: Brecht's V-effect. Bill, after all, even sells Church of Stop Shopping merchandise on his Web site ("We are all sinners!" he says). But his absurd demand is more than just a stunt: it is part of an inchoate political strategy. And the reverend is not alone.

It is New Year's Day 1994, the day the North American Free Trade Agreement goes into effect, and out of the mountains of southern Mexico walk three thousand indigenous peasants wearing black ski masks, some carrying rifles, others with merely machetes or long sticks, declaring war on the Mexican oligarchy. The "First Declaration of the Lacondon Jungle" of the Zapatista Army of National Liberation (EZLN) explains that this ragtag band of rebels are taking up arms in the struggle for political democracy and economic justice. The Zapatistas' resident poet-in-arms Subcomandante Marcos then lays out their plans. The first step is: "to advance to the capital of the country, overcoming the Mexican Federal Army, protecting in our advance the civilian population, and permitting the people liberated to elect, freely and democratically, their own administrative authorities." It's a tall order. The Mexican army is 130,000 soldiers strong, and Mexico City, the capital, is 663 very indirect miles away; the Zapatista army numbers in the low thousands and many carry only sticks. Guerrilla declarations are often full of bravado, but there's a hint of something else going on here. The "Fifth Order" gives another clue: "We ask for the unconditional surrender of the enemy's headquarters, before we begin combat, in order to avoid any loss of life."[60] Did I forget to mention the size and armament of the Zapatista "army"?

After capturing and briefly controlling the old colonial town of San Cristobel de las Casas, the EZLN retreated into the jungle, but over the next decade the Subcomandante continued to issue communiqués. Sometimes his missives were straightforward commentary on the state of the struggle or responses to Mexican politics, but other communiqués were dreamlike allegorical tales, narratives in which politics were intertwined with dialogues between Marcos and a little beetle dubbed Durito, or made into surreal metaphor with commentary provided by a fictional character named Old Don Antonio. Drawing from indigenous folk tales and contemporary magical realist literature, these revolutionary communiqués amuse as much as demand, suggest as much as state, imagine as much as plan. They are dreamscapes, not rational political communication. It was no surprise when the guerrilla leader, in an interview with the novelist Gabriel García Márquez, proclaimed that "*Don Quixote* is the best book of political theory."[61]

The imagination (and wit) of the Zapatistas is not limited to their communiqués. Six years after the EZLN demonstrated their formidable army to the world, they unveiled their "air force" against a Mexican army encampment. Guerrillas wrote notes to soldiers asking them to put down their weapons, then folded these notes into hundreds of paper airplanes and flew them over the razor wire encircling the armed camp.

For all its whimsy, this politics of dreams and spectacle seems to have had real effect on the ground. Within the decade the Zapatistas, in fact, made it to the capital, where over 250,000 Mexicans gathered in Mexico City's main plaza to greet them. And, more important, the ruling party of Mexico, which had controlled the country for almost a century, was forced (with little loss of life) to hold honest elections . . . and lost.[62] As Marcos writes, "In our dreams we have seen another world."[63]

There is much that separates the Church of Stop Shopping and the Zapatistas. The former is a political performance piece playing to an urbane audience, the latter an armed guerrilla struggle of indigenous peasants in southern Mexico. But they do share something: the reach of their imagination. The dreams of Martin Luther King Jr.—his early ones, at least—were reasonable, responsible, and realizable.[64] The reactions to a totalizing reality circle back on themselves, creating antidreams of resistance. But the dreams of Reverend Billy and Subcomandante Marcos move past the real: they are absurd, irrational, and seemingly impossible. In brief, *they remain dreams*. It is no coincidence that Reverend Billy has become well known among young progressive activists in the United States in recent years, nor that Subcomandante Marcos has inspired dissenters worldwide, for what they articulate in their fanciful musings resonates with the political experience of this generation of activists: when it is impossible to think of an alternative, then maybe the solution is to think about the impossible.[65] As their Parisian forebears wrote on the walls of their city in 1968: *Soyons réalistes, demandons l'impossible!* Be realistic, demand the impossible!

There is a potential problem with a progressive politics based on impossibilities. Setting up unrealizable expectations can absolve one from the responsibility of ever having to make anything concrete happen. To say, for example, that absolute equality and universal justice are the goal and anything less is unacceptable easily becomes a recipe for political disengagement if, in the name of the pure ideal, one refuses to engage in politics that bring just a tad more justice or a smidgen of equality. The "unconditional impossible demand," points out the radical theorist Slavoj Žižek, becomes an excuse for remaining marginal, a permanent opposition that counts on the established powers to run the system as it busies itself issuing inoperable ideals. What appears as a sort of political idealism is, as Žižek concludes, merely a "radical refusal to assume responsibility for Power."[66] Thus all this dreaming may merely give a new face to the old, problematic character of progressives. The liberals who insist upon a politics based only on rationality and reason, and the radicals who demand the impossible with no compromise, are left in the same state: political impotence coupled with a sense of moral superiority. An unattractive combination.

But I'm not worried about this, for there is a difference between a politics that insists on meeting the unconditional impossible and the politics of ethical spectacle. Ethical spectacle, as I argued earlier, must always root itself in the real. This seems paradoxical when speaking of absurd dreams of a world without consumption or revolution without bloodshed, but it makes sense if one remembers that an ethical spectacle becomes real insofar as it presents itself as what it actually is. Likewise, political dreams, if they are ethical, are always recognizable as dreams. They may promise magical transformation, but they also frankly acknowledge that they are magical. The problem with the "unconditional impossible demand" is not that it is a dream, but that it is a fantasy masquerading as a possible reality.

Between the real and the fantasy lies the dream. The dream, if it is truly a dream, is never meant to be realized. This is why it is not a contradiction for Reverend Billy to pitch products on his Web site or join in campaigns to get Starbucks to sell Fair Trade coffee while preaching "the revolution of no shopping." This is why the Zapatistas can act as if they are a mighty force without worrying that the truth will be revealed. The dreams each offers up are so patently absurd that there is little danger that they would be taken as blueprints to follow or a final state to reach. Instead they are meant to inspire and to guide, to be a lodestone to orient a political compass. Unlike programs or plans, or even the reasonable dreams of progressives past, the dream politics I am describing offer no comfort or quietude in claims of realization, nor disillusion or disengagement from disappointment in a goal not met. Still, these dreams become an ephemeral focal point around which to build identity, community, and solidarity.[67] They also provide something that progressives currently and desperately lack: inspiration and direction.

If my description seems a bit fuzzy, or perhaps even feverish, it is because the concept is, too. These dream politics have less in common with the clear and ordered platforms of political parties than they do with the hyperbolic manifestos of the avant garde. "What is the use of looking behind at the moment when we must open the mysterious shutters of the impossible?" asked the Futurists. "I don't want words that other people have invented," the Dadaists proclaimed. "When will we have sleeping logicians, sleeping philosophers?" André Breton wrote in his *Manifesto of Surrealism*. "I would like to sleep, in order to surrender myself to

the dreamers . . . in order to stop imposing, in this realm, the conscious rhythm of my thought."[68] It is this sort of political imagination that inspired Reclaim the Streets in New York City to make
the ridiculous demand on one of our broadsheets for "great feasts
of public space."[69]

Like a poem, political dreams are not meant to be read literally.
A poem suggests what its language will never allow it to communicate. It evokes rather than describes. Furthermore, a poem
encourages the reader to move past the words on the page into a
space not yet defined; it builds an edifice to show what's not there.
It may be true that "poetry makes nothing happen" as W.H. Auden
suggests. Yet, he reminds us, that

>   . . . it survives
> In the valley of its making where executives
> Would never want to tamper, flows on south
> From ranches of isolation and the busy griefs,
> Raw towns that we believe and die in; it survives,
> A way of happening, a mouth.[70]

In his eulogy to the Irish poet and radical William Butler Yeats,
Auden denies the political efficacy of poetry in one line while hint-
ing at its effect with his next. Poetry carves out untampered val-
leys and articulates unutterable fears and hopes. It makes nothing
happen but is a way of happening itself. It demands to be spoken,
and from this mouth its imaginings flow out to a wider sea.

Politics can work in much the same way. In *Empire* Hardt and
Negri argue that the diffuse but totalizing power and reach of
Empire are "outside measure" and therefore the struggle against
this system must be the same; a movement "beyond measure" is
necessary to move past Empire entirely.[71] Their politics of immea-

surability is an apt description for the politics I am describing. As historian Robin D.G. Kelley suggests in his book *Freedom Dreams*, "Progressive social movements do not simply produce statistics and narratives of oppression; rather, the best ones do what great poetry always does: transport us to another place, compel us to relive horrors and, more importantly, enable us to imagine a new society."[72] For in refusing to be reduced to rational plans, political dreams—like poems—ask us to imagine something truly new.[73]

Spectacle, however, is not merely a dream imagined or a poem read, but often a "happening" that people in one way or another participate in.[74] Activists today, as I have mentioned previously, often insist that the goals of their politics be expressed in the means of their protest. Social movement scholars like Barbara Epstein call this "pre-figurative politics," a process in which the vision of the future is prefigured in the practices of the present, thereby erasing the distinction between means and ends.[75] The early civil rights movement in the United States was an instance when organizers, black and other, tried *within* their organizing to create an interracial "beloved community" as a model of what they were trying to create *through* their organizing.

Another example is the "spokescouncil" meetings of the contemporary anticorporate globalization movement. These meetings, which have their roots in antinuke protests of the 1980s, are decision-making bodies used to hammer out strategies and plan mass demonstrations. They work like this: individuals come together in small affinity groups. Each affinity group elects a spokesperson who attends a large council meeting made up of "spokes" from all the affinity groups. Here a consensual decision is hammered out. The representative then returns to her affinity group with the larger group's decision and again tries to reach consensus. These meetings are supposed to "prefigure" the type of radical democracy of another world that is possible; a model of a nonhierarchical participatory democracy that is the antithesis to the powerful nonrepresentational bodies like the World Trade Organization the activists are protesting. The problem, as anyone who has sat through these interminable meetings can tell you, is that prefigurative politics don't work. The meetings are long and boring and tend to be dominated by those with the loudest voices and most extreme ideologies. Decisions are made less by the collective and more by those individuals still standing at the end of the marathon meetings. And the next day, at the demonstration, protesters do more or less what they want, covering over this failure of consensus with the euphemism "diversity of tactics." If this is the future, I want nothing of it.

It is no mystery why prefigurative politics are a failure. The same people who imagine this new world of democratic cooperation live the rest of their lives in a world of individualistic competition. They are not prefiguring a new world as much as acting out the old one in a hopeful new setting. It is the old problem of totality: there is no outside. But prefigurative politics *do* work in another way. The experience of doing something different, whether it is acting out a new form of democracy in a meeting or taking over a street for a dance party, is a transformative experience in itself. The new setting transforms the old action. The spokescouncil meetings are a failure as an effective demonstration of radical democracy, but the experience of acting within and through this "failure" teaches volumes about the possibilities and pitfalls of nonhierarchical models of politics.[76] As activist and theorist David Graeber points out: "It's one thing to say 'Another World Is Possible.' It's another to experience it, however momentarily."[77]

As it is with these meetings, it is with spectacle (and one might argue that these meetings are largely a form of spectacle). It is the process of engaging in a space imagined that we can imagine new spaces. It is through this acting out of a dream that new dreams can arise. Dancing in the streets with Reclaim the Streets is not the revolution, but participation in such an act gives a feel for what the revolution might be about. Supporting Cindy Sheehan in her vigil to meet the president may not directly result in stopping the war in Iraq, but going through the process gives a glimpse of a political system where the concerns of grieving mothers are paramount. Ideology is not something just thought about—in fact, it works best when it's not thought about at all. The dominant ideology remains dominant because it is lived through. Similarly, counterideologies work best when they are not just imagined but performed. Ethical spectacle is a dream self-consciously enacted.[78]

If "a dream enacted" sounds utopian, it is . . . and isn't. Traditionally, utopias are an ideal state (both literally and figuratively). These utopias may be theoretical, like Plato's ancient Greek *Republic*, Thomas More's sixteenth-century *Utopia*, and the model society of the future sketched by Edward Bellamy in the late 1800s in his popular *Looking Backward*. Or they might be the horrific utopias realized by the Soviet Union or Nazi Germany in the twentieth century. But in each case utopia is a realizable state. Progress has stopped, perfection has been reached, it is the end of history ("Actually existing socialism," as Joseph Stalin had the audacity to proclaim). There is, however, another definition of utopia, one that harkens back to the original meaning of the Greek *ou-topos*: no-place. It is in this vein that the poet Eduardo Galeano writes of utopia:

> She's on the horizon. . . . I go two steps, she moves two steps away.
> I walk ten steps and the horizon runs ten steps ahead. No matter

how much I walk, I'll never reach her. What good is utopia? That's what: it's good for walking.[79]

This is the goal of the ethical spectacle as well. The error is to see the spectacle as the new world. This is what both fascist and commercial spectacle does, and in this way the spectacle becomes a replacement for dreaming. Ethical spectacle offers up a different formulation. Instead of a dream's replacement, the ethical spectacle is a dream put on display. It is a dream that we can watch, think about, act within, try on for size, yet necessarily never realize. The ethical spectacle is a means, like the dreams it performs, to imagine new ends. As such, the ethical spectacle has the possibility of *creating* an outside—as an illusion. This is not the delusion of believing that you have created an outside, but an illusion that gives direction and motivation that might just get you there.[80]

I would love to give an example of the ideal ethical spectacle, one which incorporates all the properties listed above. I can't. There isn't one. The ideal ethical spectacle is like a dream itself: something to work, and walk, toward. Progressives have a lot of walking to do. We need to do this with our feet on the ground, with a clear understanding of the real (and imaginary) terrain of the country. But we also need to dream, for without dreams we won't know where we are walking to.

Progressive dreams, to have any real political impact, need to become popular dreams. This will only happen if they resonate with the dreams that people already have—like those expressed in commercial culture today, and even those manifested through fascism in the past. But for progressive dreams to stand a chance of becoming popular, they, too, need to be displayed. Our dreams do little good locked inside our heads and sequestered within our small circles; they need to be heard and seen, articulated and performed—yelled from the mountaintop. This is the job of spectacle. Spectacle is already part of our political and economic life; the important question is whose ethics does it embody and whose dreams does it express.

7. Dreampolitik

Politics today, whether one likes it or not, is not played out on the well-ordered fields of reason and rationality. Perhaps it never was. Aristotle created a *theory* of politics in which irrationality was sequestered to a few, last pages, raised solely as a warning. But Niccolò Machiavelli, who examined the *practice* of politics in his 1532 guidebook *The Prince*, understood that fantasy and desire were integral to power. Some of Machiavelli's advice on the subject is crude: the prince "ought, at convenient seasons of the year, to keep the people occupied with festivals and shows"—that is, the time-tested subterfuge of the circuses of the Roman Empire and the processions of the Church.[1] But Machiavelli also displays a more sophisticated understanding of spectacle, acknowledging that it operates not just negatively but also positively, not merely as a distraction from power but also as an attraction to it. The prince must *display*, if not actually possess, attributes like integrity and good faith that the people look for in a leader. The prince who did not understand the passions of his people would not be a prince for long, and the leader who attended to only what is, and not what things appeared to be, would lead very few not very far. The prince must be feared, to be sure, but he must also be loved by his subjects. "For it must be noted," Machiavelli writes, "that men must either be caressed or else annihilated."[2]

Machiavelli, writing in the time of the Medici, had political options open to him that—thankfully—we do not. Annihilation was an approved political method, and *The Prince* is full of examples where leaders consolidated their rule through the slaughter of a few rivals. Democracy changed this equation. Once popular rule was accepted as a principle in the eighteenth century and then as a slowly expanding practice in the centuries that followed, the assassination of a couple of key noblemen no longer worked as a path to power. Politics now rest upon public opinion and participation—or, at the very least, the passive consent—of the majority of the population. As such, the political options open in our age of popular sovereignty are either mass genocide or the public caress. The horrors of the last century (continuing into this one, sadly) are a testament that genocide still happens, but as a political tactic it tends to be frowned upon by the world community. Smart leaders have learned the art of the caress.

By raising the spirit of Machiavelli I am not suggesting that progressives embrace the brutal and duplicitous politics recommended by the favored author of five hundred years of despots. Nor am I proposing that we adopt a cynical policy of the manufacture of consent through a public relations crafted caress. But I am suggesting that we need to get our heads out of the sand and take a serious look at the political landscape that Machiavelli describes:

> It appears to me more proper to go to the real truth of the mat-
> ter than to its imagination, and many have imagined republics
> and principalities which have never been seen or known to exist
> in reality; for how we live life is so far removed from how we ought
> to live, that he who abandons what is done for what ought to be
> done, will rather learn to bring about his own ruin rather than his
> preservation.[3]

The irony here, which Machiavelli well understood, is that only the "imagined republic" is built solely upon reality. The "real truth of the matter" is that states and governments are based, in part, on imagination. Machiavelli is one of the few canonical writers on politics who understood his task not as one of creating an illusion of a world of political reason, but as one of using reason to understand a political world that depended upon illusion.

Perhaps we *ought* to live by reason alone—though I would rather not live in such a sober world. And perhaps progressives *ought* to address all their appeals in rational arguments and careful proofs; we will certainly feel better about our Enlightenment-infused selves if we do. But make no mistake: Machiavelli is right, and unless progressives acknowledge and accept a politics of imagination, desire, and spectacle, and, most important, *make it ethical and make it our own*, we will bring about our "ruin rather than preservation."

The world cannot afford this. The conservative revolution in this country has brought us war in the Middle East, alienated our allies, emboldened terrorists, eroded civil liberties, legitimated torture, hastened ecological destruction, widened the income gap, bungled domestic crises, and increased the deficit. What's astounding, given this record of signature failures (and unpopular successes), is that conservatives still set the agenda. They certainly deserve credit for their political acumen and the skill with which they employ the spectacular, just as they deserve condemnation for parading fantasy as reality. But behind a great deal of their success lies the failure of progressives. Conservatives have given us opening after opening, but with our historical reluctance to communicate in the lingua franca of spectacle and our aversion to addressing the irrational, the only sounds heard from our direction are equivocating murmurs of timid discourse and sighs of righteous indignation.

Conservatives have not attained and remained in power because they've convinced everyone that they have all the right answers. That fiction would be too hard to sustain in the face of so much evidence to the contrary. What they have done, and have done very effectively, is convince most people that there is no alternative. Sadly, they are correct. The people who pioneered the expansion of democracy, challenged corporate monopoly, built the New Deal, struggled for civil rights, and ushered in a cultural revolution are largely silent today. We have no alternatives to propose. We don't because we've distanced ourselves from our dreams.

There are good reasons why we've done this—the exhaustion or corruption of dreams past, for one. But more pressing is our fear of losing ourselves in to the delusional and dishonest fantasies that comprise so much of today's entertainment, religion, and politics. We distinguish ourselves from this immoral morass through our fidelity to the Real and the True, building an identity for ourselves as brave defenders of "Enlightenment principles and empiricism." Creating a dichotomy between the real and the imaginary, we are resolutely on the side of the former. This is a false, and debilitating, division. Embracing our dreams does not necessitate closing our eyes, and minds, to reality. Progressives can, and should, do both: judiciously study *and* vividly dream. In essence, we need to become a party of conscious dreamers.

Right now the only people flying this flag are sequestered to the far fringes of progressive politics. Some of this marginalization is of their own choice. Many of the street activists and political performers I've described in these pages are suspicious of more mainstream progressives who, in their eyes, have abandoned the utopian dreams that once directed and motivated the left. They also have contempt for the tactical (non)sense of a bumbling, fumbling Democratic Party. "At least we shut down Seattle and opened up a discussion on the politics of globalization," they brag (an estimation shared, with some concern, by the editors of the *Financial Times*).[4] Disgusted by the conciliation and incompetence of their more moderate comrades, these progressives often keep their own company.

But this marginalization is not entirely of their own making, for progressives ensconced in the center show little interest in their left flank. The Lower East Side Collective is too small, Reclaim the Streets too frivolous, the Billionaires too theatrical, MoveOn too ephemeral, Reverend Billy too silly, Apollo too earnest, *BUST* too racy, Critical Mass too chaotic, the Zapatistas too revolutionary, and the New Deal and civil rights movement too dated to appeal to a majority of citizens. There's validity to this criticism, as many of the groups I've been writing about do seem decidedly outside the main currents of contemporary politics. But they needn't be.

Here conservatives have something to teach us. In a letter to his brother in 1954, President Dwight D. Eisenhower wrote that "should any political party attempt to abolish social security, unemployment insurance, and eliminate labor laws and farm programs, you would not hear of that party again in our political history." He continued: "There is a tiny splinter group, of course, that believes you can do these things," then concludes, "Their number is negligible and they are stupid."[5] For years these "negligible" and "stupid" people, the far-right wing of Eisenhower's own Republican Party, dreamed seemingly impossible dreams: to roll back the most successful government initiative in U.S. history, the New Deal, and do away with what seemed like a foregone conclusion for the developed countries of the world, the welfare state. Today their dreams are our reality.

The Republican Party learned to look to its margins. Grover Norquist, Ralph Reed, Karl Rove, Ronald Reagan—all these men at one time might have been described as Eisenhower's "negligible" and "stupid" people, members of a "tiny splinter group" whose fringe politics guaranteed their irrelevance. They are also the very people who led the Republicans to power over the past few decades. During the same decades groups like the Democratic Leadership Council argued that the Democratic Party needed to abandon its margins and move to the center. They were successful. As a result the Democrats have virtually no connection to the aesthetic and political fringes of the progressive movement today.

It's a shame because these people—in all their marginality— have a better understanding of how the center operates than do the centrist professionals inside the Beltway. They understand the popular desire for fantasy and the political potential of dreams, and they know how to mobilize spectacle. They have a better read on the attractions of popular culture and the possibilities of harnessing this for progressive politics than the "pragmatic" center who, secure in their sense of superiority, stick to their failed script of reason and rationality. Left on their own, these sidelined activists have been busy experimenting with new forms of political organization and communication. But because of their peripheral

position, their efforts—with some notable exceptions—have been
politically inconsequential.

The Democratic Leadership Council's raison d'être is to spread
the center of liberal politics all the way to the margins of the left.
Whatever one thinks of this strategy theoretically, practically
it has been a failure. For all their bluster about being the ones
who are realistic about power and politics, they have not been
able to deliver political power to the Democrats (only a relatively
powerless president: Bill Clinton). It is time to cut our losses and
try another tack by moving the strategies, tactics, and organization of the margins to the center. This will take convincing on all
sides. Those on the margins need to take power seriously, giving
up the privileged purity of the gadfly and court jester and making peace with the dirtier aspects of practical politics: the daily
compromises that come with real governance. Those in the center
have to be open to a new way of thinking about politics that challenges some of their core beliefs about the sufficiency of judicious
study and rational discourse and the efficacy of a professionalized
politics. The centrists need to acknowledge that their model of
politics is, ironically, out of touch with the cultural center of our
society. They must be willing to dream.

Dreams are powerful. They are repositories of our desire. They
animate the entertainment industry and drive consumption. They
can blind people to reality and provide cover for political horror.
But they also inspire us to imagine that things could be radically
different than they are today, and then believe we can progress
toward that imaginary world.

I too have a dream. In my dream progressives of all stripes
work together. We don't agree on ideology or come to consensus
on policy. (While we may agree on fundamentals, we're still too far
apart on particulars.) But we learn to share a political aesthetic

that makes peace with the irrational, honors desire, and embraces spectacle. This may seem impossible, but if progressives are serious about winning, if we really want to change reality, then we have to try to do something different, together. It's a dream.

Notes

Chapter 1

1. Ron Suskind, "Without a Doubt," *New York Times Magazine*, October 17, 2004, p. 51.
2. See, for example, Molly Ivins's "The Reality-Based Environment," *AlterNet*, December 16, 2004, www.alternet.org.
3. In the spring of 2006 the streets of Paris were again choked with tear gas and clogged by protestors, but this time the students and young workers were on the streets not to overthrow the status quo, but to conserve the meager social programs still left in place. As a leader of the largest student union, the Union Nationale des Étudiants de France (UNEF), explained to a *Times* reporter: "We're not back there in '68. Our revolt is not to get more. It's to keep what we have." Elaine Sciolino, "Not '68, but French Youths Hear Similar Cry to Rise Up," *New York Times*, March 17, 2006, p. A6.
4. Galileo Galilei, cited in Lewis Mumford, *Technics and Civilization* (New York: Harcourt Brace, 1934), p. 48.
5. Thomas Paine understood this when he named his revolutionary pamphlet *Common Sense*, for he was trying to overturn the common-sense notions about government and sovereignty. As an ace pamphleteer he understood that the best way to do this was to defend his new

democratic message with the old stories of kings in the Bible—that is, practice the art of transmutation. Thomas Paine, *Common Sense*, ed. Isaac Kramnick (New York: Penguin, 1776/1983).

6. The U.S. Progressive Party at the turn of the nineteenth century was largely made up of professionals such as social workers, doctors, teachers, and engineers. These were people who fervently believed in the Enlightenment, confident that they could rationally understand and engineer society in the same way that the laws of mechanical physics could be discerned and a steam engine engineered.

7. I am hardly the first on the left to criticize the Enlightenment. This critique was central to the theories of Theodor Adorno and Michel Foucault, to name only two of the most famous. In the 1940s Adorno and his Frankfurt School colleague Max Horkheimer argued that Nazi barbarism and debased capitalist consumer culture, far from being aberrations of the Enlightenment, were instead its dialectical twin. The social and technological apparatuses to which reason had given birth were now working to undermine reason by reducing the world to things, to mere instruments "set free" for exploitation. In addition, the Enlightenment itself generated its own myth—"The world as a gigantic analytic judgment"—every bit as totalizing as the myths it was trying to do away with. In later decades Foucault brought the critique of the Enlightenment closer in, accusing it of engendering a new and intimate site of control in the guise of the autonomous reasoning subject. In such a subject, the locus of authority encompassed both body *and* mind, reason itself functioning as an internalized and thus inescapable disciplinary agent. These critiques are compelling; my own is less philosophical and more immediately political. My problem with the principles of Enlightenment and empiricism is that they don't work very well in the democratic contest for power. Theodor Adorno and Max Horkheimer, *Dialectics of Enlightenment* (New York: Continuum, 1947/1989), p. 27; nearly all of Foucault's writings carry this theme, but see Michel Foucault, *Discipline and Punish* (New York: Vintage, 1979).

8. Robert Reich, *Work of Nations* (New York: Knopf, 1991); Scott Lash and John Urry, *Economies of Signs and Space* (London: Sage, 1994); Richard Florida, *The Rise of the Creative Class* (New York: Basic Books, 2002);

Maurizio Lazzarato, "Immaterial Labor," in *Radical Thought in Italy: A Potential Politics*, ed. Paolo Virno and Michael Hardt (Minneapolis: University of Minnesota, 1996), pp. 132–47.

The importance of the "creative economy" tends to be overhyped, and cultural industries still comprise a small fraction of overall gross domestic product (GDP). However, as the service or "affective" labor sector has grown and culture has become an integral part of all production—from design to marketing—it is no exaggeration to say that our economy has become culturized.

9. Guy Debord, *Society of the Spectacle* (Detroit: Black & Red, 1977).

10. Gary Langer, "Poll: No Role for Government in Schiavo Case," ABC News poll, ABC News, March 21, 2005, www.abcnews.com.

11. Walter Lippmann, *Public Opinion* (New York: Free Press, 1922/1997), p. 158.

12. Thomas Frank, *What's the Matter with Kansas?* (New York: Metropolitan, 2004).

13. George Lakoff, *Moral Politics*, 2nd ed. (Chicago: University of Chicago Press, 2002), p. 4; Lakoff, *Don't Think of an Elephant* (White River Junction, VT: Chelsea Green, 2004), pp. 109–10. Lakoff goes as far as to suggest that these perceptions and understandings, with repeated use, forge neural pathways over time, essentially hardwiring ways of making sense into our very minds.

14. Jim Wallis, *The Soul of Politics* (New York: The New Press; Maryknoll, NY: Orbis Books, 1994), p. 45, cf. pp. 38–47; Wallis, *God's Politics* (San Francisco: HarperSanFrancisco, 2005). Another progressive religious thinker, Rabbi Michael Lerner, makes the case for something similar that he calls a "politics of meaning." Michael Lerner, *The Politics of Meaning* (Reading, MA: Addison-Wesley, 1996).

15. Aristotle, *The Politics*, trans. T.A. Sinclair (London: Penguin, 1962), p. 430.

16. Ibid., p. 475.

17. Ibid., p. 469.

18. The irrational does have its purpose in politics for Aristotle. Speaking again of music, he writes: "For the relaxation of [common persons] competitions and spectacles must be provided," reiterating and propagating the age-old wisdom of rulers that spectacle is a worthy *distrac-*

tion from real politics, suitable for placating the rabble. Aristotle, *The Politics*, p. 474.

19. For a good overview of the ways in which human passion (the "libidinal economy") has been ignored in the study of politics in general and social movements in particular, and why this is a problem, see the editor's introduction, "Why Emotions Matter," to the anthology *Passionate Politics*, ed. Jeff Goodwin, James M. Jasper, and Francesca Polletta (Chicago: University of Chicago Press, 2001).

20. Edmund Burke, *Reflections on the Revolution in France 1790* (Oxford: Oxford University Press, 1790/1993), p. 45.

21. Karl Marx and Frederick Engels, *The Communist Manifesto* (New York and London: Verso, 1848/1998), pp. 38–39.

22. P.H. Collin, *Dictionary of Government and Politics* (Middlesex, UK: Peter Collin Publishing, 1997), p. 68.

23. Jack C. Plano and Milton Greenberg, *American Political Dictionary* (Belmont, CA: Thomson Publishing, 2002), p. 76.

24. Famed radio announcer Norman Brokenshire, while reminiscing over an early assignment covering the 1924 Democratic National Convention, describes "one of the finest donnybrooks I'd ever seen. Delegation signs were banged down on opponents' heads, chairs and decorations destroyed." Brokenshire goes on to recall how his boss pulled him aside, chastised him for reporting the fight, and explained that their station "had only secured broadcast rights to the event on the distinct understanding that no disorders of any kind would be reported." Today, since political conventions are explicitly constructed for broadcast, no such directions are needed. Norman Brokenshire, *This Is Norman Brokenshire* (New York: D. McKay, 1954), pp. 47–48.

25. Janice Radway, one of the first and still the best of this cultural-consumption-as-resistance school, makes this very point. While pointing out how the reading of romance novels creates a space of self-pleasure for women conditioned to think about the needs of others, Radway underscores that the reader, "[a]lthough she may feel temporarily revived . . . has done nothing to alter her relations with others." Janice A. Radway, *Reading the Romance: Women, Patriarchy, and Popular Literature* (Chapel Hill: University of North Carolina Press, 1984), p. 85.

26. Scion USA Web site, www.scion.com.

27. William James, "The Moral Equivalent of War," *Essays in Religion and Morality* (Cambridge, MA: Harvard University Press, 1982), pp. 165 and 168–69, respectively; emphasis is the author's. The moral equivalent of war that James suggests is a conscription civil service in the line of the Civilian Conservation Corps, Peace Corps, or AmeriCorps. This civil service would be used to wage what he describes, in an unfortunate turn of phrase, as a "war against nature."

28. Neil Gabler, *Life, the Movie* (New York: Knopf, 1998). As a good left-liberal, Gabler is predictably horrified by "how entertainment conquered reality." But, like all such writers, he doesn't move past the critique into what might be done with this new state we live in.

29. Critics have made an assault on reality. Jean Baudrillard argues that our "real" has been eviscerated by simulacra—a simulation of a simulation. And Slavoj Žižek identifies our passion for the real as merely our passion for a fantasy of the real, a mythic escape from the reality of the phantasmagoria in which we live our lives. But neither theorist denies material reality per se (though Baudrillard toes the line); they argue instead that "the real" must always be understood in and through its meaning. Exactly. Jean Baudrillard, "Precession of Simulacra," in *Simulations* (New York: Semiotext(e), 1983); Slavoj Žižek, *Welcome to the Desert of the Real* (London and New York: Verso, 2002).

30. For instance, if I drop a pen, it falls, demonstrating the reality of gravity. But what we do with this reality is what I am interested in. A physical law becomes a metaphor—"What goes up must come down"—and this a way of *making sense* of the world.

31. Lippmann, *Public Opinion*, p. 10. Lippmann calls this simulation of a simulation "pseudoenvironment," predating Jean Baudrillard's use of the term "simulacra."

32. "Evolution is a fact," writes renowned biologist Richard Dawkins. "It is not a theory, and for pity's sake, let's stop confusing the philosophically naïve by calling it so." Such an assertion refutes the basic premise of conditional hypotheses which undergirds scientific research (philosophically naïve, indeed), but it is a pretty good example of the arrogance of Enlightenment ideology. Richard Dawkins, "The Illusion of Design," *Natural History*, November 2005, p. 37.

33. Poll conducted by the Pew Forum on Religion and Public Life and the Pew Research Center for the People and the Press, reported in Laurie Goldstein, "Teaching of Creationism Endorsed in New Survey," *New York Times*, August 31, 2005, p. 9.

34. Global warming deniers, so it seems, also employ the flip side to the marketing of ideas: the power to censor them. Andrew C. Revkin, "Climate Expert Says NASA Tried to Silence Him," *New York Times*, January 29, 2006, p. 1.

35. Berkowitz quoted in Andrew Rich, "War of Ideas," *Stanford Social Innovation Review*, Spring 2005, no page. Years of comparison are 2004 for Brookings (3 percent of a $39 million budget) and 2002 for Heritage (20 percent of $33 million).

36. Other progressives have begun to realize this as well. Says Don Hazen, the executive editor of the Web site AlterNet.org: "Progressives have been under the illusion that if only people understood the facts, we'd be fine. Wrong. The facts alone will not set us free. People make decisions about politics and candidates based on their value system, and the language and frames that invoke these values." Discussing the Bush team's propaganda campaign to convince America of the need for the Iraq war, John Sellers, executive director of the activist training group Ruckus Society, says, "The truth doesn't matter anymore." Sellers is not making some grand metaphysical claim but, like Hazen, rather matter-of-factly asserting that the truth is no longer *the* deciding factor in people's opinions. Hazen quoted in Lakoff, *Don't Think of an Elephant*, p. xiii; Sellers from a personal conversation with Andrew Boyd, 2003.

37. William James, *Pragmatism* (New York: Meridian Books, 1907/1955), p. 133.

38. Free, aka Abbie Hoffman, *Revolution for the Hell of It* (New York: Dial Press, 1968), p. 64. Hoffman is one of the few activists I have come across who explicitly used advertising as a model for protest. In *Revolution for the Hell of It*, he draws upon the mostly visual ad for the Dreyfus Fund (a lion walking slowly down Wall Street) to make his point that images, and mystery, are more important than words and explanations in attracting people and making a point. See pp. 83–86.

39. Michael Moore has offered $10,000 to anyone who can disprove the facts in his film. To my knowledge he has not paid anyone.

40. Frank Bardacke, "Epilogue," in Subcomandante Marcos, *Shadows of Tender Fury* (New York: Monthly Review Press, 1995), p. 264.

41. The problem for the activists of the Naramada Valley protests, and even the insurgents of the Zapatista army, is less throwing off the weight of Enlightenment history than the resurrection, reconnection, and operationalization of indigenous traditions in which the real and the fantasy, the material and the imaginary, have no fixed lines. In this, activists of the south have a distinct advantage over their comrades in the north, who must learn to transform and employ the only real culture at their disposal: commercial entertainment and advertising.

42. Alexander Stille, "The Latest Obscenity Has Seven Letters," *New York Times*, September 13, 2003, sec. B, p. 9. Stille, a respected writer on Italian fascism, attempts to clarify what fascism is and is not by distinguishing a genuine political and philosophical system from a blanket epithet used by the left to denigrate anyone or anything they don't agree with. Ironically, by tarring any political system which speaks to emotion and mobilizes myth as fascist, Stille is guilty of the same sort of simplification and stereotyping he criticizes.

43. David Solnit, telephone interview, July 8, 2002.

44. Rove cited in John Cassidy, "The Ringleader," *New Yorker*, August 1, 2005, p. 53. Rove is referencing the state of conservatism following Barry Goldwater's 1964 defeat in particular.

45. Laurie Goodstein, "Intelligent Design Might Be Meeting Its Maker," *New York Times*, December 4, 2005, sec. 4, p. 1.

46. Joseph Alvarez, "World's Elite to Debate Global Health Challenges at U.S. Summit," *Christian Today*, November 1, 2005, www.christiantoday.com.

47. Rep. John Murtha, Speech in the U.S. House of Representatives, November 17, 2005, AlterNet, November 19, 2005, www.alternet.org.

48. Walter Lippmann, *The Phantom Public* (New Brunswick, NJ: Transaction Publishers, 1924/2004), pp. 145 and 93, respectively.

Chapter 2

1. MSNBC's Bob Kurr and Fox's Josh Gibson, respectively. Cited in Rachel Smolkin, "Are the News Media Soft on Bush?" *American Journalism Review*, October/November 2003, www.ajr.org.

2. "Vegas by the Numbers," www.vegas.com.

3. Robert Venturi, Denise Scott Brown, and Steven Izenour, *Learning from Las Vegas* (Cambridge, MA: MIT Press, 1977), p. 154.

4. Walter Lippmann, *A Preface to Politics* (Amherst, NY: Prometheus Books, 1913/2005), p. 42.

5. Ronald Steel, *Walter Lippmann and the American Century* (Boston: Little, Brown and Co., 1980). Unless otherwise noted, all biographical details on Lippmann are from this source.

6. Lippmann, *A Preface to Politics*, p. 44. Using the influential 1911 vice report on "The Social Evil in Chicago" as an example, Lippmann shows how the respectable commissioners charged with investigating the problem of prostitution rarely asked the question of why men use prostitutes or why women become them. Instead, the 400-page report is filled with sanctimonious condemnations of loose morality and detailed recommendations for its repression.

7. Lippmann, *A Preface to Politics*, p. 49.

8. Borrowing the term from William James, Lippmann writes, "To find for evil its moral equivalent is to be conservative about values and radical about forms." *A Preface to Politics*, p. 52.

9. As singer Ice Cube rapped with NWA in the late 1980s: "We don't just say no. We're too busy sayin' yeah!" NWA (Niggaz With Attitude), "Gangsta Gangsta," *Straight Outta Compton*, Priority Records, 1988.

10. Lippmann, *A Preface to Politics*, p. 54.

11. Ibid., p. 127.

12. Ibid., p. 177.

13. This is Lippmann at his boldest. In other places he retreats to the Freudian orthodoxy of unruly passions that need to be civilized. For example, he writes elsewhere that "the task of politics is to understand those deeper demands and to find civilized satisfactions for them." *A Preface to Politics*, p. 54.

14. Lippmann, *A Preface to Politics*, p. 239. It is Freud's theories that Lippmann acknowledges, but the same insight was provided by his

teacher William James, who wrote of militaristic desires that "they are its first form, but that is no reason for supposing them to be its last form." William James, "The Moral Equivalent of War," in *Essays in Religion and Morality* (Cambridge, MA: Harvard University Press, 1982), p. 171.

15. Lippmann, *A Preface to Politics*, p. 191. Lippmann soon came to distrust the irrational in politics, considering it no longer a power to be respected and harnessed but instead an intractable impediment to democratic rule. His experience serving in a propaganda bureau during World War I (a rival outfit to George Creel's Committee on Public Information) and his peacetime observations of how principles of propaganda were being used to sell soap, publicize movie stars, sway public opinion, and garner votes convinced Lippmann that people could easily be manipulated—their consent manufactured—by those skillful in the arts of symbol and spectacle. Therefore, he reasoned, democracy could not be left in the hands of everyday people, and political decisions must made by dispassionate experts (conveniently, like himself). Observing how people's fantasies were being assembled and redirected by leaders for individual gain, Lippmann abandoned his earlier hopes that leaders could learn from popular desire to create a more responsive politics. Lippmann's disillusionment led him to conflate what *had* happened with what *could* happen. Walter Lippmann, *Public Opinion* (New York: Free Press, 1922/1997) and *The Phantom Public* (New Brunswick, NJ: Transaction Publishers, 1924/2004).

16. Jeff Rickert, telephone interview, August 25, 2005.

17. John Podesta, speech at Wayne State University, Detroit, Michigan, February 9, 2004.

18. Jeff Rickert, telephone interview, August 25, 2005.

19. "Report on the Apollo Project for Good Jobs and Energy Independence," Annual Report, Apollo Alliance, January 2005; Jeff Rickert, telephone interview, August 25, 2005.

20. "A Forward Looking Strategy for Change," Apollo Alliance Web site, www.apolloalliance.org.

21. Quoted in Ruth Rosen, "Aiming for the Moon," *San Francisco Chronicle*, September 1, 2003, p. B7.

22. The Radio Act of 1927, which became the basis for all future communications regulation in the United States, stipulated that the award

and renewal of broadcast licenses is conditioned upon serving "the public interest, convenience or necessity." This intentionally vague phrase has been contested ever since. Public-minded communications advocates define "public interest" as information that is necessary for an informed public, while commercial broadcasters define "public interest" as whatever interests the public—that is: whatever gets high ratings. Needless to say, commercial interests have, by and large, carried the debate.

23. Lippmann, *A Preface to Politics*, p. 87.
24. Ibid., p. 86.
25. Marc Cooper, *The Last Honest Place in America* (New York: Nation Books, 2004), p. 7.
26. Casino developer and Las Vegas resident Mark Advent plans to build "East Village," a "retail-office-entertainment" center based upon New York City's neighborhood of the same name, near the Las Vegas airport. Because this is Vegas, this "East Village" will include the West Village's Washington Arch, Chelsea's Meatpacking District, and Midtown's Diamond District. "It's not an exact replica," Advent explains, preferring to think of it as an "homage." Steven Kurutz, "East Village West," *New York Times*, August 14, 2005, City Section, p. 6.
27. Baudelaire elaborates:

> Woman is quite within her rights, indeed she is even accomplishing a kind of duty, when she devotes herself to appearing magical and supernatural. . . . It matters little that the artifice and trickery is known to all, so long as their success is assured and their effect always irresistible.

Charles Baudelaire, "In Praise of Cosmetics," in *The Painter of Modern Life* (London: Phaidon, 1863/1965), p. 33.
28. Susan Sontag, "Notes on 'Camp,'" in *Against Interpretation* (New York: Picador, 1966), pp. 280 and 275, respectively.
29. The Billionaires were mentioned in the *New York Times*, *Washington Post*, *Time*, CNN, Fox, NPR, ABC, CBS, as well as local swing-state venues such as the *St. Petersburg Times*, *Cleveland Plain Dealer*, *Pittsburgh Post-Gazette*,

Detroit Free Press, Akron Beacon Journal, and the *Las Vegas Review-Journal.* They also had a starring role in an Art Spiegelman cartoon in the *New Yorker.*

30. Adapted from an interview, "Andrew Boyd, Cultural Activist and Founder, Billionaires for Bush," Gothamist.com, October 29, 2004.

31. The Center for Business and Economic Research, University of Las Vegas, "Metropolitan Las Vegas Tourism Statistics," cber.unlv.edu/tour .html; "Vegas by the Numbers," www.vegas.com.

32. Cooper, *The Last Honest Place in America,* pp. 202–03.

33. Bertolt Brecht, "Emphasis on Sport," in *Brecht on Theatre,* trans. John Willett (New York: Hill and Wang, 1964), p. 8.

Chapter 3

1. Tim Winter, quoted by Bethany McLean, "Grand Theft: Sex, Lies and Videogames," *Fortune,* August 8, 2005, www.fortune.com.

2. *Grand Theft Auto: San Andreas,* PlayStation2, Rockstar Games, 2004.

3. McLean, "Grand Theft: Sex, Lies and Videogames"; staff, "NPD: $9.9 Billion Worth of Console Games Sold in 2004," *Gamespot,* January 18, 2005, www.gamespot.com. The $9.9 billion number is for console games only and does not reflect the figures for personal computers, which, if included, would no doubt push this impressive number even higher.

4. Alex Pham, "Hidden Sex Scenes Spark Furor over Video Game," *Los Angeles Times,* July 21, 2005, p. 1; staff, "NPD: $9.9 Billion Worth of Console Games Sold in 2004."

5. "Rockstar's *Grand Theft Auto: San Andreas* Shoots Its Way to #1 in Video Game Rentals," PR *Newswire,* November 4, 2004.

6. Seth Schiesel, "Video Game Known for Violence Lands in Rating Trouble Over Sex," *New York Times,* July 21, 2005, p. 1.

7. John Gaudiosi, "Pirated Games on Net Before Shelves," *Toronto Star,* November 2, 2004, p. D6.

8. Sigmund Freud, *Civilization and Its Discontents* (New York: W.W. Norton, 1930/1984); Aristotle, *Poetics* (New York: Penguin, 1997). *Desublimation* is a term used by Herbert Marcuse; see, for example, *An Essay on Liberation* (Boston: Beacon Press, 1969), p. 35.

9. There are user-made "mods" available on Web sites devoted to the game to make CJ appear white (or at least bleached). A mod was even posted to transform the protagonist into a caricature of Fred Durst, the white lead singer of Limp Bizkit. But based on the number of downloads, these race modifications were much less popular than features like new car models, neon packs for under-lighting, and, of course, "Hot Coffee." Source for mods: www.gtagarage.com.

10. NWA (Niggaz With Attitude), "Gangsta Gangsta," *Straight Outta Compton*, Priority Records, 1988.

11. Norman Mailer, "The White Negro: Superficial Reflections on the Hipster," *Dissent*, IV, 1957.

12. The young Stokely Carmichael realized this, too. The 1965 campaign in Selma, Alabama, which started with the assembly of well-dressed school teachers at the Selma courthouse, ended with the future Black Panther leading the call-and-response: "What do you want? Black Power!" and effectively hijacking the civil rights movement by articulating open rebellion.

13. The other people in attendance at Senator Clinton's press conference were David Walsh, the president of the National Institute of Media and Family; Norman Rosenberg, head of Parents' Action for Children; Kristen Stewart of the Family Violence Prevention Fund; and Mary Bissell, a fellow at the New America Foundation. Secure in their dark vision of human nature, these critics remain surprisingly unaware of what actually happens in video games and thus why people enjoy them so much. Some of this ignorance is startling. After the stock speeches decrying the impact of mediated sex and violence on our society, a reporter asked the personages assembled, "Have you guys played the game *San Andreas*?" It was a revealing moment. In rapid succession the panelists answered:

> —Played it? No. No.
> —I haven't.
> —I haven't.
> —I try to play some of these games with my kids, but they beat me so bad and so fast that I've decided it's not worth the effort. So I really—I haven't.

Press conference with Senator Hillary Clinton, "Calling for FTC Investigation into Video Games," July 14, 2005, *Federal News Service*.

14. Rap music and video games are even ahead of progressives in seeing the popular potential of identification with political rebellion. Rockstar Games, the parent company of *Grand Theft Auto*, flirted with radical politics with their game *State of Siege*, which was loosely modeled on the protests in Seattle. (Any political—and popular—potential, however, was short-circuited by reducing politics of rebellion to spray-painting slogans on walls and smashing store windows.) About the same time NWA was breaking new musical ground glorifying the thug life in Los Angeles, their neighbor (and genuine ex-thug) Ice-T was rapping critically about Reagan's foreign and domestic policies, the Coup was singing about socialism up in the Bay Area, and the New York group Public Enemy already had a hit political song, "Fight the Power." It is a positive sign that the progressive radio network Air America recruited Chuck D, the lead singer of Public Enemy, to be an on-air host. (Flavor Flav, Chuck D's partner in Public Enemy, was tapped to star on MTV's freak show *The Surreal Life*—proving, once again, that the inchoate possibilities of cultural rebellion can lead to celebrity freakdom as easily as rebel politics.)

15. *GTA/SA* is what the industry calls a "third-person shooter"—that is, you identify with CJ from a short distance away: riding shotgun, floating a little above and a little behind the character. Other popular games, like *Doom*, my dear old *Wolfenstein 3D*, and most auto racing and flight simulation games are "first-person shooters," bringing you literally inside the head and body of the character, an even closer identification with the "Other." *GTA/SA* offers the option to toggle into this perspective at certain points in the game.

16. Gonzalo Frasca, "Sim Sin City: Some Thoughts About *Grand Theft Auto 3*," *Game Studies* 3, no. 2 (December 2003), no page.

17. Katie Salen and Eric Zimmerman, *Rules of Play: Game Design Fundamentals* (Cambridge, MA: MIT Press, 2004), p. 95.

18. Johan Huizinga, *Homo Ludens* (Boston: Beacon Press, 1955), p. 57.

19. "The deepest *Grand Theft Auto* yet" is how Greg Stewart, game reviewer for the gaming channel G4 (yes, there is a cable channel devoted solely

to gaming) described GTA/SA. Greg Stewart, "*Grand Theft Auto: San Andreas* Review," G4 Web site, July 26, 2005, www.G4tv.com.

20. Source for these mods: www.gtagarage.com.

21. For a good overview of the "Hot Coffee" controversy, see Robert MacMillan, "'San Andreas' Rocks the 'Righteous,'" *Washington Post*, July 27, 2005, www.washingtonpost.com.

22. Janet H. Murray, *Hamlet on the Holodeck* (Cambridge, MA: MIT Press, 1997), p. 152.

23. The freedom of agency in a game like *Grand Theft Auto* has expanded to such a great degree that game scholars have begun to argue that player agency has transcended authorial control, something Celia Pearce calls "emergent authorship." Celia Pearce, "Emergent Authorship: The Next Interactive Revolution," *Computers & Graphics* (2001); Cindy Poremba, "Against Embedded Agency: Subversion and Emergence in *GTA III*," unpublished manuscript, 2003.

24. Dan Houser quoted on *GTASanAn*, August 28, 2005, www.gtasan andreas.net/overview.

25. Greg Costikyan, "Fifty Cents Don't Buy Me No Token," blog entry, March 3, 2005, www.costik.com/weblog.

26. In 2005 Universal Pictures released a $70 million movie based on the popular first-person shooter *Doom*. In an attempt to simulate the gaming experience, the directors position the audience behind the eyes of characters on the screen. However, because this is a movie with a fixed storyline, spectator agency and range of exploration are nil, thus taking away a major part of the attraction of video games. Predictably, the movie failed at the box office. As one reviewer commented, "There is one element of the movie that invites interactivity: talking back to the screen about the stupidity of the characters, the screenwriters, the director, and yourself for wasting $10 and two hours." James Berardinelli, "*Doom* Review," *Reelviews: Berardinelli Sees Film*, www.movie-reviews .colossus.net.

27. Routine game playing, like seemingly everything else, has been off-shored to China. An estimated 100,000 young gamers play online games in China, racking up virtual rewards, and then sell their supercharged avatars to Western gamers who desire the extra gaming

power yet don't have the time to build up their virtual resumes themselves. At first glance this seems a refutation of my "the game's the thing" thesis. I don't think it is. It may be a despicable practice (and one frowned upon by most players), but it is not about cheating to win, but about cheating to compete at a higher level, bypassing the humdrum tedium of collecting enough rewards for your online character to have agency. Buyers want to get to the fun part of the game faster. David Barboza, "Ogre to Slay? Outsource It to the Chinese," *New York Times*, December 9, 2005, p. 1.

28. One of the largest of these solicitation firms is DialogueDirect, which began fund-raising for Greenpeace in Austria in 1995 and now has offices and nonprofit "partners" in the United Kingdom, Ireland, Australia, and the United States; www.dialoguedirect.com.

29. Julie Traves, "Walk on By, Avert Your Eyes," *Toronto Globe and Mail*, July 16, 2005, no page.

30. For a fuller discussion of Reclaim the Streets/New York City see Stephen Duncombe, "Stepping off the Sidewalk: Reclaim the Streets/NYC," in *From Act Up to the WTO*, ed. Benjamin Shepard and Ronald Hayduk (London and New York: Verso, 2002), pp. 215–28.

31. *Do or Die* #6, Summer 1997; reprinted as "The Evolution of Reclaim the Streets" on the RTS/London Web site: www.gn.apc.org/rts/evol.htm; John Jordan, "The Art of Necessity: The Subversive Imagination of Anti-Road Protest and Reclaim the Streets," in *DIY Culture*, ed. George McKay (London and New York: Verso, 1998).

32. William Etundi, telephone interview, July 10, 2002.

33. Barbara Epstein, "The Politics of Prefigurative Community: The Nonviolent Direct-Action Movement," in *Reshaping the US Left: Popular Struggles in the 1980s*, ed. Mike Davis and Michael Sprinker (London and New York: Verso, 1988); Barbara Epstein, *Political Protest and Cultural Revolution* (Berkeley: University of California Press, 1991).

34. Ganz cited in Gregory Dicum, "Green: The Sierra Club at a Crossroads," *SFGate*, August 31, 2005, www.sfgate.com. For a similar critique see also Michael Schellenberger and Ted Nordhaus, "The Death of Environmentalism: Global Warming Politics in a Post-Environmental World," released at an October 2004 meeting of the Environmental Grantmakers Association.

35. Dan Houser quoted in Seth Schiesel, "Gangs of New York," *New York Times*, October 16, 2005, sect. 2, p. 1.

36. Salen and Zimmerman, *Rules of Play*. The importance of "transformative play" was first brought to my attention by Robert Jones in his unpublished manuscript, "Machinima: Transformative Play in 3D Game-Based Filmmaking," 2005.

37. Guy Debord, "Report on the Construction of Situations and the International Situationist Tendency's Conditions of Organization and Action," 1957, in *Situationist International Anthology*, ed. and trans. Ken Knabb (Berkeley: Bureau of Public Secrets, 1981), p. 24, cf. Debord's "Theory of the Dérive," 1958, also in *Situationist International Anthology*, pp. 50–54.

38. See Naomi Klein's excellent response to this criticism of the globalization protests in "The Vision Thing: Were the DC and Seattle Protests Unfocused or Are Critics Missing the Point?" in *From Act Up to the WTO*, ed. Benjamin Shepard and Ronald Hayduk (London and New York: Verso, 2002).

39. Salen and Zimmerman, *Rules of Play*, p. 97; in their exaltation of the inefficient in games, the authors are drawing upon the work of Bernard Suits in his book *The Grasshopper: Games, Life and Utopia* (Toronto: University of Toronto Press, 1978).

40. MoveOn press release, "'Child's Pay' Ad by Charlie Fisher Wins MoveOn.org Voter Fund's 'Bush in 30 Seconds' TV Ad Contest," MoveOn Voter's Fund, January 12, 2004. Needless to say, the novelty of such popular participation in creating an advertisement created its own media, broadcasting the message of MoveOn to far more people than were ever able to actually watch the ad.

41. Matthew A. Crenson and Benjamin Ginsberg, *Downsizing Democracy: How America Sidelined Its Citizens and Privatized Its Public* (Baltimore: Johns Hopkins University Press, 2002).

42. As the feminist Judith Butler argues in her case for sexual pleasure within an acknowledged sexist and homophobic society,

> If sexuality is culturally constructed within existing power relations, then the postulation of a normative sexuality that is "before," "outside," or "beyond" power is a cultural impossibility and

a politically impractible dream, one that postpones the concrete and contemporary task of rethinking subversive possibilities for sexuality and identity within the terms of power itself.

Judith Butler, *Gender Trouble: Feminism and the Subversion of Identity* (London and New York: Routledge, 1999), p. 40.

Chapter 4

1. Neal Postman, in "Consuming Images," part of Bill Moyers's PBS series *The Public Mind*, 1989. Postman is referring specifically to the ad I begin this chapter with. While the ad is now more than fifteen years old, its formula is still employed by McDonald's today. The characters, slogans, and settings change, but the promise remains the same.

2. John Berger, *Ways of Seeing* (London: BBC/Penguin, 1972).

3. Juliet Schor, *The Overworked American* (New York: Basic Books, 1992). According to a recent study on "Generation and Gender in the Workplace" (New York: Families and Work Institute/American Business Collaboration, 2005), younger, college-educated workers are less likely to be "work centric" than the previous baby boomer generation and more interested in free time and time with their family. This concern seems to cross class as well: Caterpillar workers went on strike in the mid-1990s for, among other things, the right to refuse working overtime. Unfortunately, the workers lost.

4. Such an appeal for stasis or deprivation may serve all sorts of perverse psychological needs, feeding into the unhealthy progressive penchant for marginalization, but using politics for therapy is bad faith.

5. Stuart Elliot, "Nowadays, It's All Yours, Mine or Ours," *New York Times*, May 2, 2006, pp. C1, 6. The senior vice president of Coca-Cola quoted is Katie Bayne.

6. The newest McDonald's slogan—"I'm lovin' it"—pushes personal identification to its apogee as the "you" watching becomes the "I" of the voice of the advertisement.

7. ". . . and there are families," Thatcher added, almost as an afterthought. Interview with Margaret Thatcher, *Women's Own Magazine*, October 31, 1987.

8. This is, essentially, Neal Postman's reading of the very same McDonald's advertisement in *The Public Mind*. I am in full agreement with Postman's analysis; we differ only on the nature of the solution.

9. In the voiceover to Jason Simon's video *Production Notes: Fast Food for Thought* (1986), an anonymous advertising executive instructs the production house shooting an advertisement for Mars candy bars: "The editing of the pictures draws an equation for us between life's best things and Mars. And the music does the same . . . making the case simply by listing Mars ingredients among life's other best things as if this inclusion were the most natural in the world." The resulting advertisement is an almost avant garde montage of images and jump cuts between candy and people at play, people in love, and so on.

10. Ad agency DDB of Chicago designed Bud Light's "Real Men of Genius" series that scored so highly in the 2004 Clio awards. Since then Budweiser has continued to run this campaign with slight modifications, continued accolades, and the same basic (dis)associative formula.

11. The venerable advertising agency J. Walter Thompson lowers their sights even further. "Time is the new currency," they proclaim in their 2006 "client manifesto," explaining that they are "in the new business of buying people's time." Whatever—whatever—grabs and holds the viewer is what defines a successful ad as "the more time spent, the more valuable the advertising becomes." Advertising becomes an empty spectacle. "Time. The New Currency," J. Walter Thompson client manifesto, 2006, www.jwt.com.

12. Martin Luther King Jr., "Why Jesus Called a Man a Fool," delivered at Mount Pisgah Missionary Baptist Church, Chicago, IL, August 27, 1967.

13. Martin Luther King Jr., "Beyond Vietnam," delivered at Riverside Church, New York, NY, April 4, 1967. King was not the first progressive who drew our attention to hidden lines of connection. Karl Marx, in his analysis of "The Fetishism of the Commodity and Its Secret" in *Capital*, reminds us that the items that appear to us in the marketplace as free-floating commodities have deep social histories: the stories of the hands that produced them, the social links between producers and consumers, the interdependent social system that all of us have

built. It is capitalism, Marx argues, that has cloaked these associations, burying the social history of the product under the surface of the commodity: "transform[ing] every product of labour into a social hieroglyphic"; hiding from humanity "the secret of their own social product." This process of erasure and substitution is one in which Madison Avenue has played a leading role, replacing the living lineage of materials, labor, and exchange with an autonomous and "phantasmagoric" product personality. Pontiac breeds excitement! Karl Marx, *Capital*, vol. 1 (London: Penguin Books, 1992), p. 16.

14. Michael Schellenberger and Ted Nordhaus, "The Death of Environmentalism: Global Warming Politics in a Post-Environmental World," released at an October 2004 meeting of the Environmental Grantmakers Association; Peter Teague's quote is on p. 4.

15. Lower East Side Collective flyer, New York, circa 1997.

16. Alice Meaker Varon, LESC strategy session, 1997.

17. Jim Wallis, *The Soul of Politics* (New York: The New Press; Maryknoll, NY: Orbis Books, 1994), p. 231. The anecdote is also repeated in Joyce Hollyday, "Living the Word," *Sojourners*, September/October 1995.

18. Kevin Roberts, *Lovemarks: The Future Beyond Brands* (New York: PowerHouse Books, 2004), pp. 74, 85.

19. William Banning, cited in Stuart Ewen, *PR!: A Social History of Spin* (New York: Basic Books, 1996), p. 194.

20. American Apparel also plays the other side, advertising its products and building its brand image with soft-core pornographic pictures of some of its young and attractive female workers modeling its clothes.

21. George Lakoff, *Don't Think of an Elephant* (White River Junction, VT: Chelsea Green, 2004); Lakoff also makes the argument in more depth in *Moral Politics*, 2nd ed. (Chicago: University of Chicago Press, 2002).

22. In 2003, $245.48 billion was spent on advertising, including all commissions as well as art, mechanical, and production expenses. *Advertising Age's FactPack 2005* (New York: Advertising Age, 2005), p. 14.

23. Stuart Elliot, "No More Same-Old," *New York Times*, May 23, 2005, p. C1. Ad spending has bounced back from its low in 2001 but has not regained its previous growth rate.

24. Carl Johnson quoted in Elliot, "No More Same-Old," p. C8.

25. Sheena Bizarre, "Train Parties," in *Cultural Resistance Reader*, ed. Stephen Duncombe (New York and London: Verso, 2002), pp. 116–17.
26. Stuart and Liz Ewen, *Channels of Desire* (New York: McGraw-Hill, 1982).
27. Berger continues:

> Either he then becomes fully conscious of the contradiction and its causes, and so joins the political struggle for a full democracy which entails, amongst other things, the overthrow of capitalism; or else he lives, continually subject to an envy, which, compounded with his sense of powerlessness, dissolves into recurrent day-dreams.

It is Berger's solution to the problem of advertising addressing unrealized political desires that makes his analysis so useful. He is not just arguing for a "critical reading" of advertisements, except insofar as such a reading leads to social change. His goal is not to limit, regulate, or even abolish advertising. Instead he is calling for the abolition of the very conditions that generate the emotions that give advertising its power (a concept he borrows from Karl Marx's "On the Jewish Question"). Here Berger jumps the divide from the impotent negation of the critic and aligns himself with those who wish to fundamentally change the world. Berger, *Ways of Seeing*, p. 148.

28. The sublimation of utopian desire into consumer purchase is well analyzed by, among others, Stuart Ewen in his groundbreaking book on the early history of advertising, *Captains of Consciousness*, and Frederic Jameson in his essay "Reification and Utopia in Mass Culture." The latter writes that "works of mass culture cannot be ideological without at one and the same time being implicitly or explicitly Utopian as well: they cannot manipulate unless they offer some genuine shred of content as a fantasy bribe to the public." This utopia, as Jameson explains, also negates what it posits. It "strategically arouses fantasy content within careful symbolic containment structures which defuse it. . . ." Or, as I would suggest, it denies utopia only to then hold out the promise that it can be delivered with the next purchase or act of spectatorship. Stuart Ewen, *Captains of Consciousness* (New York: McGraw-Hill,

1976); Frederic Jameson, "Reification and Utopia in Mass Culture," in *Signatures of the Visible* (London and New York: Routledge, 1979), pp. 28 and 24, respectively.

Chapter 5

1. Walter Lippmann, "Blazing Publicity," *Vanity Fair*, September 1927, reprinted in *Primary Documents*, no. 2, 1999, ed. Stephen Duncombe and Andrew Mattson, no page.
2. "What was Britney thinking?" was a question asked on air so frequently by *The Insider* host Pat O'Brien that it became the butt of a joke on *Saturday Night Live*.
3. *People*'s profit: *Advertising Age's FactPack* 2005 (New York: Advertising Age, 2005), p. 37.
4. Leo Braudy, *The Frenzy of Renown* (New York: Vintage, 1986), pp. 42–43. Like many ancient heroes, Alexander, as the son of the king of Macedonia, began his life at the top of the social hierarchy. In addition, Alexander acted out his heroics for those elevated few who would write and record history. He also played to the morale of his lesser-born troops, but here his performance was decidedly less successful: they mutinied and ended his march east.
5. Joshua Gamson, *Claims to Fame* (Berkeley: University of California Press, 1994), pp. 25, 27.
6. "Fashion Police," *Us*, May 30, 2005, pp. 102–3.
7. This is akin to Marx's solution regarding the freedom of religion—that is: to be truly free in matters religious, including freedom *from* religion, you must address the material conditions that give rise to these spiritual manifestations: poverty, powerlessness, and inequality. Karl Marx, "On the Jewish Question," in *The Marx-Engels Reader*, 2nd ed., ed. Robert C. Tucker (New York: W.W. Norton, 1978), pp. 26–52.
8   Three thousand dollars per night. "The Romance Heats Up!" *Star*, May 30, 2005, pp. 12–13.
9. "Ellen Goes Glam," *Us*, May 30, 2005, p. 28; "Heidi and Seal Tie the Knot," *Celebrity Living*, May 30, 2005, no page.

10. Tom Gliatto and Kwala Mandel, "Greetings from Nick and Jessica's USO Tour," *People*, May 9, 2005, pp. 62–65.
11. In this way celebrity culture also speaks to our anxieties about class, allowing a peek at the other side of the growing class divide while assuring us—through our intimacy with this world—that it is not really another side at all.
12. Braudy, *The Frenzy of Renown*, p. 30.
13. "Stars—They're Just Like Us!" *Us*, May 30, 2005, pp. 30–31. This is a regular feature in *Us*.
14. "Diva or Down-to-Earth," *Life & Style*, May 30, 2005, pp. 84–85. Divas like Ashlee Simpson have expensive pet carrier luggage; down-to-earth stars like Teri Hatcher use cash machines on the street.
15. Corrine Barraclough, "At Home with Paris and Paris," *Celebrity Living*, May 30, 2005, p. 48.
16. "Does the Shoe Fit?" *Life & Style*, June 20, 2005, p. 68.
17. If the Nazis could subsidize and organize holidays through their *Kraft durche Freude* (Strength Through Joy) program, and today low-cost trip packages are provided by Wal-Mart Vacations™, why shouldn't a progressive party be able to deliver something similar? In early 2006 the liberal radio network Air America ran a promotion that promised their listeners a chance to win a Caribbean cruise. No doubt this frivolity horrified some on the left, but I see it as an encouraging sign. You can't challenge celebrity culture by scolding people and insisting that they embrace the real (or the left's nostalgic fantasy of the real), but we can provide a real substitute for the fantasy of leisure that is vicariously experienced through celebrity culture.
18. Leo Braudy points out that while heroes predated Alexander the Great, he was the first figure to self-consciously cast himself in that role, drawing upon Greek familiarity with the *Iliad* and the battles of Achilles to wrap his own feats in the mantle of recognized greatness. Alexander began his campaign to conquer the known world by restaging the conquest of Troy. The city had lost strategic worth long before but it still held symbolic value, for in conquering Troy Alexander inserted himself—favorably—into the story of the *Iliad* and, by extension, entered the pantheon of classic Greek heroes and gods. He also made sure that

all his glories were properly glorified by hiring Aristotle's nephew Callisthenes as his official "publicist-historian," only later to have him murdered (celebrity journalists take heed!). Braudy, *The Frenzy of Renown*, pp. 42–43.

19. Daniel Boorstin, *The Image* (New York: Vintage, 1961/1992), p. 74. Hollywood may be the epicenter of celebrity, but it's a mistake to equate even the act of acting with celebrity. There are great actors who shun celebrity, while Paris Hilton, the star of the moment, is by all accounts an atrocious actor. Paris, however, is quite accomplished at making a scene.

20. For example, see Dorothea Lange's migrant farm families series done for the FSA and the WPA murals of Maxine Albro, Victor Arnaytoff, Ray Bertrand, Malellet (Harold) Dean, Clifford Wight, et al., in San Francisco's Coit Tower.

21. Naomi Klein, "Reclaiming the Commons," talk given at the Center for Social Theory and Comparative History, UCLA, in April 2001, reprinted in *A Movement of Movements*, ed. Tom Mertes (London and New York: Verso, 2004), p. 222.

22. I am not the first to argue for the necessity of intimate community for participatory politics. Aristotle makes the case for just such community in book seven of his *Politics*. Walter Lippmann, on the other hand, argues that it is partly the scale of modern, mass democracy that makes democracy impossible. Returning to the positive, John Dewey in his book-length critique of Lippmann's thesis, *The Public and Its Problems* (Athens, OH: Ohio University Press, 1927/1980), insists that intimate political discussion is both possible in and necessary for mass democracy.

23. Karl Marx, "Contribution to the Critique of Hegel's *Philosophy of Right*: Introduction," in *The Marx-Engels Reader*, p. 63.

24. *In Touch*, May 30, 2005, cover.

25. "Renee Zellweger: Why She Rushed into Marriage," *Star*, May 30, 2005, pp. 46–49.

26. "In the Know," *In Touch*, February 27, 2006, p. 22.

27. Maxine Page, "Is the Wedding Off for Good?" *Star*, May 30, 2005, pp. 52–53.

28. *Inside TV*, May 23, 2005, pp. 26 and 20, respectively. Patrick Dempsey is "resident hunk" on the TV drama *Grey's Anatomy*, and Rob Mariano and Amber Brkich were losers in the reality TV show *Amazing Race* but deemed an attractive enough couple to snag their own reality special: *Rob and Amber Get Married*.

29. Gamson, *Claims to Fame*, p. 45.

30. Occupational Employment Statistics (OES) survey, 2001, Bureau of Labor Statistics, Department of Labor.

31. Quoted in Stuart Ewen, *PR! A Social History of Spin* (New York: Basic, 1996), pp. 255–56.

32. Ibid, p. 255.

33. George W. Bush, "The Economy," radio address, September 4, 2004, www.whitehouse.gov/news/releases/2004/09/20040904.html.

34. BUST circulation figures from 2004 compiled by Curtis Circulation and Subscription; 91 percent of readers surveyed have reported that "BUST is their favorite magazine"; www.bust.com.

35. *BUST*, June/July 2005.

36. Debbie Stoller, telephone interview, March 6, 2006.

37. There are the readers' polls and star spottings which can be e-mailed to the magazines, but this "communication" is not with celebrity but with the media, and it is eventually cycled back to the reader as content.

38. "Poll Results," *In Touch*, May 30, 2005, p. 93.

39. Gamson, *Claims to Fame*, p. 178.

40. This can be true for the video games I discuss in Chapter 3 as well. If all goes to hell you can merely reset and begin the game again. There are no irreversible consequences, and thus no real stakes. However, I still hold that one can adopt the *form* of video games (and celebrity culture, advertisements, and Las Vegas) while altering the consequences. To recall again William James: we need to move the point.

41. Benjamin's full quotation reads thus:

    The growing proletarianization of modern man and the increas-ing formation of masses are two aspects of the same process.

208 Notes

Fascism attempts to organize the newly created proletarian
masses without affecting the property structure which the
masses strive to eliminate. Fascism sees its salvation in giving
these masses not their right, but instead a chance to express
themselves. The masses have a right to change property relations; Fascism seeks to give them an expression while preserv-
ing property. The logical result of Fascism is the introduction of
aesthetics into political life.

What an ethical spectacle attempts to do is reverse the fascist equation by politicizing (political) aesthetics—that is, demonstrating the
political character of the spectacle and opening it up for examination,
debate, and participation. This is what I believe Benjamin is advising
in the cryptic last line of his essay when he writes that "communism
responds by politicizing art." Walter Benjamin, "The Work of Art in the
Age of Mechanical Reproduction," in *Illuminations*, ed. Hannah Arendt
(New York: Schocken, 1936/1969), p. 242.

Chapter 6

1. Thanks to Astra Taylor for her insight into this. For elaboration
   on how the specter of the Nazis has limited our understanding of
   the politics of un-reason, see Rey Chow, *Ethics After Idealism*
   (Bloomington: Indiana University Press, 1998), p. 14; also Michel
   Foucault, "Power and Strategies" in *Power/Knowledge* (New York:
   Pantheon, 1980).
2. Siegfried Kracauer, "The Mass Ornament," in *The Mass Ornament:
   Weimar Essays*, trans. and ed. Thomas Y. Levin (Cambridge: Harvard
   University Press, 1995), p. 77.
3. Malcolm Gladwell, "The Cellular Church," *New Yorker*, September 12,
   2005, pp. 60–67.
4. The Situationists had a great fondness for Las Vegas, recognizing
   as early as 1953 its potential as a site "set apart for free play." Ivan
   Chtcheglov, "Formulary for a New Urbanism," in *Situationist International*

Anthology, ed. and trans. Ken Knabb (Berkeley: Bureau of Public Secrets, 1981), p. 4.

5. Guy Debord, "Report on the Construction of Situations and on the International Situationist Tendency's Conditions of Organization and Action," in *Situationist International Anthology*, p. 24.

6. Katie Salen and Eric Zimmerman, *Rules of Play: Game Design Fundamentals* (Cambridge, MA: MIT Press, 2004).

7. For a more thorough discussion of the role of irony in dissenting culture, see the section on "Irony" in Stephen Duncombe, *Notes from Underground: Zines and the Politics of Alternative Culture* (New York and London: Verso, 1997), pp. 145–48.

8. Adolf Hitler, *Mein Kampf*, cited in David Welch, *The Third Reich: Politics and Propaganda*, 2nd ed. (London: Routledge, 2002), p. 11.

9. Mikhail Bakhtin, *Rabelais and His World*, trans. Helene Iswolsky (Bloomington: Indiana University Press, 1988), p. 7. Bakhtin continues, "[C]arnival does not know footlights in the sense that it does not acknowledge any distinction between actors and spectators."

10. George Mosse, *The Nationalization of the Masses* (Ithaca: Cornell University Press, 1975), p. 205.

11. Rudolf Hess, 1927, cited in Ian Kershaw, *The "Hitler Myth"* (Oxford: Oxford University Press, 1987), p. 27. Hess continues, "The great popular leader is similar to the great founder of a religion: he must communicate to his listeners an apodictic faith."

12. Cf. Carlo Ginsburg, *The Cheese and the Worms*, trans. John and Anne Tedeschi (Baltimore: Johns Hopkins University Press, 1980) for what happens when a semiliterate peasant in the sixteenth century gets his hands on a Bible and makes the "wrong" reading.

13. Umberto Eco, *The Open Work*, trans. Anna Cancogni (Cambridge, MA: Harvard University Press, 1989), p. 12.

14. Cf. Richard Rorty, *Contingency, Irony, Solidarity* (Cambridge: Cambridge University press, 1989).

15. Eco, *The Open Work*, p. 19, author's emphasis.

16. See www.critical-mass.org, as of October 18, 2005. For a thorough, albeit partisan, overview of the history and politics of Critical Mass, see *Critical Mass: Bicycling's Defiant Celebration*, ed. Chris Carlsson (Oakland,

CA: AK Press, 2002). Within this collection is an excellent piece on Critical Mass in New York City by Ben Shepard and Kelly Moore, "Reclaiming the Streets of New York," pp. 195–203.

17. Hugh D'Andrade, Critical Mass flyer, San Francisco, circa 1993, reprinted on www.scorcher.org/cmhistory/traffic.html.

18. L.M. Bogad, "Tactical Carnival: Social Movements, Demonstrations, and Dialogical Performance," 2005, unpublished manuscript, p. 5.

19. Chris Carlsson, Jim Swanson, Hugh D'Andrade, Kash, Nigel French, Beth Verdekal, Kathy Roberts, et al. "How to Make a Critical Mass: Lessons and Ideas from the San Francisco Experience," 1994, reprinted on www.scorcher.org/cmhistory/howto.html.

20. Ibid.

21. There was good reason to be suspicious of agents provocateurs. In the winter of 2005 it was revealed that the NYPD regularly placed undercover agents in demonstrations as purposefully provocative participants. Critical Mass, it was reported, was a favorite site for intervention. Jim Dwyer, "New York Police Covertly Join in at Protest Rallies," *New York Times*, December 22, 2005, p. 1.

22. Open spectacles are also open to their context: physical, historical, and social. For Critical Mass this means adapting to the geography of the city where it occurs, the history of bicycling in the locale, and the character of its citizens and its authorities. Critical Mass in bike-friendly Amsterdam takes on a different character than in New York, with its famed aggressive drivers and increasingly intolerant police. For example, faced with steady and aggressive police harassment in 2005, Critical Mass in New York City became critical *masses*. In an effort to confuse the police, cyclists gathered at multiple places around the city and played a game of find-the-mass, coming together and breaking off into minimasses as the situation warranted.

23. The term "bell curve of meaning" is Andrew Boyd's. In recent years Boyd has worked extensively with viral organizations like Billionaires for Bush and is acutely aware of both the promise and problems of staying "on message" while allowing for creative autonomy.

24. Mosse, *The Nationalization of the Masses*.

25. Ibid., p. 117.

26. A similar claim for fantasy as fact appears in this 1940 statement from Joseph Goebbels to filmmakers and critics: "Films in which Jews appear are not to be labeled as anti-Jewish. We want it to be made perfectly clear that such films are not determined by any tendentious considerations, but *reflect historical facts as they are*." Quoted in Welch, *The Third Reich*, p. 99, emphasis mine.

27. Susan Sontag, "Fascinating Fascism," *New York Review of Books*, February 6, 1975, no page. Quotes from Riefenstahl are also from this source.

28. Jason Simon, *Production Notes: Fast Food for Thought*, 1986.

29. Michael Schudson calls this "capitalist realism": "It does not claim to picture reality as it is but reality as it should be—life and lives worth emulating." Michael Schudson, *Advertising: The Uneasy Persuasion* (New York: Basic, 1984), p. 215.

30. Simon, *Production Notes*.

31. Bertolt Brecht, "A Short Orangum for the Theatre," nos. 29 and 26, respectively, in *Brecht on Theatre*, trans. John Willett (New York: Hill and Wang, 1964), pp. 188, 187.

32. Rousseau continues on the same page: "The more I think about it, the more I find that everything that is played in the theater is not brought nearer to us but made more distant." [25] This is but one of Rousseau's complaints about the theater. Given his Enlightenment penchant for Reason (even as this essay marks his break with d'Almbert, Voltaire, and the l'*Encyclopédie* crowd), it is not surprising to find that his major grievance is that the stage caters to, and inflames, the less-than-virtuous "immoderate passions" of its audience, passions which are then carried outside the playhouse to influence the "moral order." That this theory contradicts his earlier one on the vicarious release of virtue appears not to bother the philosopher. [See sections IV and V, pp. 34–57.]

Rousseau, interestingly, also has his own version of the ethical spectacle. After condemning the theater for page upon page, he posits an alternative: unstaged, participatory festivals:

Plant a stake crowned with flowers in the middle of a square; gather the people there, and you will have a festival. Do better yet; let the spectators become an entertainment to themselves;

make them actors themselves; do it so each sees and loves himself in the others so that all will be better united. [126]

That this resonates with my own ideas of a participatory spectacle should be obvious; where we differ is on illusion. Rousseau can see no illusion that is not also delusion (or "deception," as he calls it). I believe—along with Brecht—that illusion can be self-conscious and therefore not deceptive. Jean-Jacques Rousseau, *Politics and the Arts: The Letter to M. d'Alembert on the Theatre*, trans. Allan Bloom (Ithaca, NY: Cornell University Press, 1758/1968).

33. Brecht, "Alienation Effects in Chinese Acting," in *Brecht on Theatre*, pp. 91–98. Brecht popularized the term *epic theatre* (first using it to describe his technique in 1926), but he did not invent it. The term had been used to describe the work of the director, and Brecht's collaborator, Erwin Piscator in the early 1920s.

34. Brecht, note to "Emphasis on Sport," in *Brecht on Theatre*, p. 8.

35. Brecht, "A Short Orangum for the Theatre," no. 3, in *Brecht on Theatre*, pp. 180–81; cf. "Emphasis on Sport," pp. 6–8.

36. John Leland, "Why America's Hooked on Wrestling," *Newsweek*, February 7, 2000, p. 46; Michael J. Weiss, Morris B. Holbrook, and John Habich, "Death of the Arts Snob?" *American Demographics*, June 2001, p. 4.

37. The director Michael Moore—whether consciously or not—employs many of Brecht's V-effects in his documentaries by including himself in the frame and the story, making the story of being denied access to sources part of the film, and interjecting classic Brechtian comic relief at key moments. In *Fahrenheit 9-11*, for example, Moore rents an ice cream truck to drive around the Capitol building while reading the U.S. Constitution aloud through the truck's PA system. Brecht would have approved.

38. Brecht, "A Short Orangum for the Theatre," no. 43, p. 192.

39. As Herbert Marcuse wrote about the clowning of activists like Abbie Hoffman in the 1960s, which got under the skin of the establishment (and many serious-minded radicals), "The rebels revise the desperate laughter and the cynical defiance of the fool as means for demasking the deeds of the serious ones who govern the whole."

Herbert Marcuse, *An Essay on Liberation* (Boston: Beacon Press, 1969), p. 64.

40. Billionaires for Bush, "Legislation: A Lucrative Investment," Billionaires for Bush Investment, Letter no. 23, 2004.

41. Billionaires for Bush, flyer circa 2003–04.

42. David Frankel, "Hunger Artist: David Frankel on Brian Tolle," *ArtForum*, Summer 2002, no page.

43. Brecht, "A Short Orangum for the Theatre," no. 71, in *Brecht on Theatre*, p. 203.

44. John Cox and Allen Forkum, "Show of Grief," August 14, 2005, www.coxandforkum.com; Limbaugh quote reported in Frank Rich, "The Swift Boating of Cindy Sheehan," *New York Times*, August 21, 2005, no page.

45. Associated Press, "Grieving Mother's War Protest Gaining Momentum," August 11, 2005, www.cnn.com; in this article Sheehan is compared to Rosa Parks by Reverend Lennox Yearwood, a leader of the Hip-Hop Caucus.

46. Michael A. Fletcher, "Cindy Sheehan's Pitched Battle," *Washington Post*, August 13, 2005, p. 1.

47. Jean Baudrillard, "Precession of Simulacra," in *Simulations* (New York: Semiotext(e), 1983).

48. Doug McAdam, "The Framing Function of Movement Tactics," in *Comparative Perspectives on Social Movements*, ed. Doug McAdam, John D. McCarthy, and Mayer N. Zald (Cambridge: Cambridge University Press, 1996), p. 348. McAdam goes on to point out that the "strategic dramaturgy," so effective in the early years of the civil rights movement, became much more difficult to employ once the movement moved north and confronted foils less willing than Bull Conner to play the role of archvillain.

49. Walter Lippmann, *Public Opinion* (New York: Free Press, 1922/1997), p. 104.

50. Kershaw, *The "Hitler Myth,"* pp. 187–99.

51. Martin Luther King Jr., "I Have a Dream," speech delivered in Washington, D.C., August 28, 1963.

52. McAdam, "The Framing Function of Movement Tactics," especially pp. 347–48 on "ideational framing."

53. "Now We Can Finally Put Civil Rights Behind Us," *The Onion*, November 10–16, 2005, p. 1.

54. "The Great Refusal" was a term popularized by Herbert Marcuse, but the term may have originated with Alfred N. Whitehead or even earlier with André Breton. The brilliance of Marcuse is that he acknowledged the problem of totality, held out the possibility of the Other as outside, understood the inherent potentiality of negative thinking and resistant refusal, *and* championed the importance of radical imagination, or, in his wonderful phrasing, "the faith in the rationality of imagination"—all at the same time. Marcuse, *An Essay on Liberation*, p. 26.

55. Jean Baudrillard, "The Masses: The Implosion of the Social in the Media," trans. Marie Maclean, *New Literary History* 16, no. 3 (Spring 1985), pp. 577–89.

56. Michael Hardt and Antonio Negri, *Empire* (Cambridge, MA: Harvard University Press, 2000), p. 211.

57. Bill Talen, quoted in Jason Grote, "The God That People Who Do Not Believe in God Believe In," in *Cultural Resistance Reader*, ed. Stephen Duncombe (London and New York: Verso, 2002), pp. 365–66. The sermon cited was recorded at a "shopping intervention" at the Disney Store in Times Square in 1999. Bill, however, has also used this sermon in his church services.

58. Bill Talen, reply to "rave on," November 1, 2005, www.revbilly.com.

59. Bill Talen, *What Should I Do if Reverend Billy Is in My Store?* (New York: The New Press, 2003), p. 24.

60. General Command of the EZLN, "First Declaration of the Lacandon Jungle," January 2, 1994, reprinted in *Our Word Is Our Weapon*, ed. Juana Ponce de León (New York: Seven Stories Press, 2001), pp. 13–15.

61. Continuing, Marcos explains to Márquez, "When we got into Marx and Engels we were thoroughly spoilt by literature, its irony and humor." Subcomandante Marcos, "The Hourglass of the Zapatistas," interview with Gabriel García Márquez and Roberto Pombo, in *A Movement of Movements*, ed. Tom Mertes (London and New York: Verso, 2004), p. 14.

62. The ruling Institutional Revolutionary Party (PRI) lost the presidential elections of 2000, albeit to the conservative National Action Party (PAN).

63. Subcomandante Marcos, "Thanks to the NGOs for their Protection,"
    March 1, 1994, in *Shadows of Tender Fury*, trans. Frank Bardacke, Leslie
    López, et al. (New York: Monthly Review Press, 1995), p. 163. As Naomi
    Klein writes, "In the Zapatistas, we have not one dream of a revolution,
    but a dreaming revolution." Klein, "The Unknown Icon," March 3, 2001,
    www.nologo.org.

64. By the end of his life King's dreams demanded the "unreasonable": in-
    ternational solidarity, economic equality, global peace, an end to colo-
    nialism, and a challenge to capitalism. Read, for example, "Why Jesus
    Called a Man a Fool," delivered at Mount Pisgah Missionary Baptist
    Church, Chicago, IL, August 27, 1967, and "Beyond Vietnam" delivered
    at Riverside Church, New York, NY, April 4, 1967. King was assassi-
    nated the year following these impossible dreams.

65. "[E]mancipatory politics always consists in making seem possible pre-
    cisely that which, from within the situation, is declared to be impos-
    sible. " As a radical, the French Maoist Alain Badiou understands the
    necessity of thinking outside the possible; however, I am less confident
    and comfortable with the idea of the realizable impossible, preferring
    instead the impossible as a guide rather than a destination. Alain
    Badiou, *Ethics*, trans. Peter Hallward (London and New York: Verso,
    2001), p. 121.

66. Slavoj Žižek, *The Ticklish Subject* (London and New York: Verso, 1999),
    pp. 233, 235. It is not that your typical progressive has no desire, only
    that he has a repressed desire for impotency so that things do not
    change and his hard-won (or rather, lost) identity as outsider is not
    challenged.

67. In this way political dreams serve the same function as Georges Sorel's
    "myth of a general strike": an organizing myth which focuses and mo-
    tivates the proletariat in its struggle for power. As Ernesto Laclau and
    Chantal Mouffe explain:

    It matters little whether or not the general strike can be real-
    ized: its role is that of a regulating principle, which allows the
    proletariat to think of the *mélange* of social relations as orga-
    nized around a clear line of demarcation; the category of totality,
    eliminated as an objective description of reality, is reintroduced

as a mythical element establishing the unity of the workers' consciousness.

Ernesto Laclau and Chantal Mouffe, *Hegemony and Socialist Strategy* (London and New York: Verso, 1985), p. 40.
68. F.T. Marinetti, *The Futurist Manifesto*, 1909; Hugo Ball, *Dada Manifesto*, 1916; André Breton, *Manifesto of Surrealism*, 1924. Breton continues:

> Why should I not grant to dreams what I occasionally refuse reality, that is, this value of certainty in itself which, in its own time, is not open to my repudiation? Why should I not expect from the sign of the dream more than I expect from a degree of consciousness which is daily more acute? Can't the dream also be used in solving the fundamental questions of life?

69. "Mayor Giuliani's Quality of Life Campaign hinges on his definition of 'quality of life.' Is this yours?" Reclaim the Streets/New York City flyer, circa 1998.
70. W.H. Auden, "In Memory of W.B. Yeats," in *Collected Poems*, ed. Edward Mendelson (New York: Vintage, 1991), p. 248.
71. Hardt and Negri, *Empire*, section on "Virtualities," especially p. 357.
72. Borrowing the term from the black surrealist Aimé Césaire, Kelley calls this integral but underappreciated aspect of social movements "Poetic Knowledge." Robin D.G. Kelley, *Freedom Dreams: The Black Radical Imagination* (Boston: Beacon Press, 2002), p. 9.
73. In this way these political dreams resonate with religious prophesy: "Prophetic spirituality can offer a vision for . . . transformation. Through stories and parables, instead of blueprints and ideologies, we hope to point the way toward a different kind of future." Jim Wallis, *The Soul of Politics* (New York: The New Press; Maryknoll, NY: Orbis Books, 1994), p. 47.
74. "Is there a possibility that in enacting a conscious spectacle we catch a glimpse of new paradigms of truth?" my Fantasy Reäl co-conspirator Jeremy Varon rhetorically asks, reminding me that the ethical spectacle must be experienced as much as imagined. Varon, personal correspondence, July 28, 2005.

75. Barbara Epstein, *Political Protest and Cultural Revolution* (Berkeley: University of California Press, 1991).

76. At a spokescouncil meeting one learns about the value of solidarity over individual preference, since nothing gets done unless the group can come to a consensus. Conversely, one also learns about the coerciveness of "groupthink" and the pressure put on individuals to conform when their dissent can hold up a decision. One develops ideas about the value of actively engaging in decision-making processes, as those who participate vigorously at meetings and stay late into the evening are the ones whose voices are heard the loudest, just as one realizes that such "democratic" bodies can discriminate against those who don't have the free time or confidence to participate at this level.

77. David Graeber, "The New Anarchists," in *A Movement of Movements*, p. 214; cf. Stephen Duncombe, "The Poverty of Theory: Anti-Intellectualism and the Value of Action," *Radical Society* 1, vol. 30 (2003). Graeber is more optimistic than I am about the immediate efficacy of these models of decision making.

78. "The opposite of the rationality of the Real, or its closed circuit of Fate . . . is the act itself," Slavoj Žižek writes, channeling in equal measure the psychoanalyst Jaques Lacan and the revolutionary Vladimir Lenin. This is an act, he continues, "which intervenes in the very rational order of the Real, changing—restructuring its co-ordinates—an act is not irrational; rather, it creates its own (new) rationality." For Žižek the only way out of the totality (of the Freudian superego, capitalist hegemony, Marxist teleology) is to act, without full knowledge, without knowing exactly where one is going to land. This is the way out of the straitjacket of a reality that tells you the extent of what is possible and in so doing limits all possibility. Thus the act that seems absurd from the standpoint of our present reality stretches the limits of what we can imagine as reasonable . . . and realizable. The absurd dreams of the ethical spectacle make room for exactly such acts. Slavoj Žižek, *Revolution at the Gates* (London and New York: Verso, 2002), p. 243.

79. Eduardo Galeano, "Window on Utopia," in *Walking Words* (New York: W.W. Norton, 1995); reprinted in *The Nation*, June 12, 1995, p. 829.

80. "Escaping is the quest for the marvelous," wrote the French philoso-

pher Emmanuel Levinas, arguing that the desire for escape is the very essence of the human condition. This is not an escape into a well-chronicled fantasy of celebrity life or an articulated, ordered utopia, which, being defined in advance, is no real escape at all. For Levinas the destination of the escape is unknown. That it is a place never reached is not a sign of deficiency or lack; it is the impulse to escape itself which must be appreciated as part of our being. Emmanuel Levinas, *On Escape*, trans. Bettina Bergo (Stanford: Stanford University Press, 1935/2003), p. 53, cf. pp. 58–63.

Chapter 7

1. Niccolò Machiavelli, *The Prince*, trans. Luigi Ricci (New York: New American Library, 1532/1952), p. 113.
2. Ibid., p. 37.
3. Ibid., p. 84.
4. "The protesters are winning. They are winning on the streets. Before long they will be winning the arguments. Globalization is fast becoming a cause without credible arguments." *Financial Times*, August 17, 2001, cited in *We Are Everywhere*, ed. Notes from Nowhere (London and New York: Verso, 2003), p. 503.
5. Letter to Edgar Newton Eisenhower, November 8, 1954, Presidential Papers of Dwight David Eisenhower, Document #1147.

Index

fantasy: in climate of fear, 7–8; co-existence of reality and, 9–10; in entertainment, 13; popular desire for, 181; in religion, 12–13
Farm Security Administration, 21, 109
feminism, 118–20
Fenton Communications, 153
Financial Times, 180
Finnegans Wake (Joyce), 135
fireside chats, 21, 115–18
"First Declaration of the Lacondon Jungle," 165
Fisher, Charlie, 75
Flavor Flav, 196n14
Florida, Richard, 185n8
Foucault, Michel, 161, 185n7, 208n1
Fox News Network, 8, 43
framing issues, 10
Frank, Thomas, 9
Frankel, David, 150
Frasca, Gonzalo, 60
freedom, in game playing, 62–65
Freedom Dreams (Kelley), 171, 216n72
French Revolution, 21
French Terror, 26
The Frenzy of Renown (Braudy), 204n4, 205n12, 206n18
Freud, Sigmund, 33, 35, 52, 54, 191nn13–14, 217n78
From Act Up to the WTO (Shepard and Hayduk, eds.), 198n30, 199n38
fun, 92
fundamentalists, 13
The Futurist Manifesto (Marinetti), 216n68
Futurists, 169

Gabler, Neil, 17, 188n28
Galeano, Eduardo, 173–74
Galileo Galilei, 3–4, 9
game playing, 51–77; and activism, 67–70, 73–76; appeal of, 54; freedom in, 62–65; in politics, 65–67, 70–72; popularity of, 52–54; rebellion in, 56–59; role playing in, 54–56

Gamson, Joshua, 121, 204n5, 207n29
Gandhi, Mahatma, 70
gangsters, 55–56
Ganz, Marshall, 71–72
Gap (store), 108, 115
García Márquez, Gabriel, 166, 214n61
Gender Trouble (Butler), 200n42
Geneva Convention, 28–29
Gibson, Josh, 191n1
Ginsberg, Benjamin, 76
Ginsburg, Carlo, 209n12
Giuliani, Rudy, 67
globalization movement, 159–60
God's Politics (Wallis), 186n14
Goebbels, Joseph, 26, 156, 211n26
Gold Star Families for Peace, 153
Goldwater, Barry, 190n44
gossip, 113–15, 120–21
Graeber, David, 172
Grand Theft Auto, 52–57, 59–64, 72–73, 76–77
The Grasshopper (Suits), 199n39
Gray Lady. See *New York Times*
Great Depression, 96, 115
Greenpeace, 66
Grey's Anatomy (television show), 207n28
Grote, Jason, 214n57
guilt, 82

Hamilton, Alexander, 12
Hamlet on the Holodeck (Murray), 64
Hardt, Michael, 163, 170–71
Hatcher, Teri, 205n14
Hazen, Don, 189n36
Hegemony and Social Strategy (Laclau and Mouffe), 215n67
Heritage Foundation, 19
Hess, Rudolph, 134
Highlander Institute, 21
Hilton, Paris, 107, 206n19
Hip-Hop Caucus, 213n45
hippies, 21
Hitler, Adolf, 26, 132, 134, 144